As I read through *Picking [...]* after my senior year in c[ollege ...] wrote to tell me that our [...] [sh]e [h]ad met someone new whom she intended to marry. For weeks, I'd get sick to my stomach when I tried to eat. I did whatever I could to avoid being alone. I dreamed about happier times and awakened in the morning wishing I could go on dreaming. I wondered if I would ever love anyone again.

I wish I'd had Lou Priolo's book back then to help me get my focus back where it belonged—on God's Word and His perfect plan for my life. God used that breakup in my life to help me see that the woman I loved had replaced Him and had become an idol in my life. Ultimately, He used that trial as He does with all trials in our lives—to perfect us and make us more like Christ. That's what this book is all about. Whether you've experienced being abandoned by someone who once promised "till death do us part," or you feel empty inside because someone you thought would always be there has left you, God is your strength! As you read through this book, you'll find the hope, the peace, and the joy that God has promised are the fruit of a growing relationship with Him.

—**Bob Lepine,** cohost, FamilyLife Today

Here you have a book about a problem that no one wants to acknowledge exists: the breakup of Christian relationships. With his typical straightforward, God-centered approach, Priolo has assembled 31 studies that will help you get to the heart of your sorrow. These thoroughly biblical, thoughtfully practical, Christ-honoring studies will help you regain your perspective and see your Savior: He's a Suffering Servant offering grace to His suffering children.

—**Elyse Fitzpatrick,** author, *Idols of the Heart,*
Overcoming Fear, Worry, and Anxiety

Relationships bring us the greatest joy in life . . . and the greatest pain. Lou Priolo has done a masterful job of applying God's Word to the anger and agony that flow from broken relationships. He also shows us how to find healing and hope through Jesus Christ so that we can go on to love others more deeply and freely than we ever imagined.

—**Ken Sande,** president, Peacemaker Ministries

Do you know someone who has experienced the pain of a broken relationship? Is that person nursing loneliness and resentment instead of getting on with the rest of his or her life? Maybe that someone is you. If so, Lou Priolo's book is full of practical, solidly biblical advice that will help you move past the hurt to be the kind of person God wants you to be. *Picking Up the Pieces* addresses topics like fear, loneliness, forgiveness, and self-pity. The author writes in an engaging style that blends just the right amount of humor with the unapologetic proclamation of God's Word. I strongly recommend it.

—**James MacDonald,** senior pastor, Harvest Bible Chapel

Picking Up the Pieces addresses a real counseling issue (the breakup of romantic relationships) in a remarkable way. In 31 short chapters (each designed to be read on a different day of the month), Lou Priolo helps hurting people learn to apply the Bible to the specific issues common to such breakups. Practical, devotional, and most of all biblical, this book should be in every counselor's toolbox.

—**Jay E. Adams,** author, speaker, seminary professor

As the biblical counseling movement continues its rapid growth in size and maturity, it is encouraging to see a growing library of practical counseling aids such as this. Lou Priolo has once again tackled a specific issue with insight and depth that can shave weeks off the time required for counseling the heartbroken person.

If someone you love has abandoned you, you can find helpful biblical suggestions for dealing with the anger, hurt, bitterness, and sense of loss in the studies Lou has provided. I suggest reading and digesting a chapter a day for 31 straight days of intensive self-confrontation. Do the assignments; make the commitment of time and energy. At the end of that time, you may find that you are well on your way toward healing.

I suspect that many biblical counselors will be assigning this book in the years ahead.

—**Ed Bulkley,** president, International
Association of Biblical Counselors

Picking Up
the Pieces

Picking Up the Pieces

Recovering from Broken Relationships

Lou Priolo

P&R
PUBLISHING
P.O. BOX 817 • PHILLIPSBURG • NEW JERSEY 08865-0817

For clarity, some of the quotations from Puritan authors and from Charles Spurgeon contained in this volume have been slightly modified (rephrased into modern English). The pronouns "he" and "she" and "him" and "her" are used interchangeably.

Italics within Scripture quotations indicate emphasis added.

Holy Bible image © istockphoto.com / Dawn Hudson
Penny image © istockphoto.com / James Trice

Printed in the United States of America

P&R ISBN: 978-1-59638-380-7

To Jay E. Adams,
one of the greatest reformers of the twentieth century.

Thank you for all you have taught me,
for exemplifying faithfulness, compassion, and courage,
and for being such a benediction to the church of Jesus Christ.

Contents

Foreword   9

Acknowledgments   11

Introduction: Your Achin', Breakin' Heart   13

1. How Can I Mend My Broken Heart?   17

2. Have You Tossed Those Lovin' Feelings?   23

3. How Do Fools "Fall in Love"?   29

4. Only *Love* Can Break a Heart?   33

5. Can't I Stop Loving You?   39

6. Love Isn't Blue   45

7. Why Are You Lonesome Tonight?   51

8. There Goes My Security Thing   57

9. Is Your Imagination Running Away with You?   63

10. It's Not the End of the World   71

11. What Good Comes to the Brokenhearted?   77

12. I *Can* Get Used to Losing You   81

13. I Just Called to Say, "I *Don't* Love You!"   87

14. Love Be Tender   93

15. Won't Be Cruel   97

CONTENTS

16. Yesterday Wants More   105

17. Will I Still Love You Tomorrow?   109

18. I Say a Little Prayer and Supplication with Thanksgiving   115

19. I'm Nobody Till Somebody Loves Me   123

20. Misheard It through the Grapevine?   129

21. Won't Look Back   135

22. It's Your Party   141

23. Who Can You Turn To?   149

24. Suspicious Mines   155

25. Isn't That a Shame?   161

26. Devoted to Who?   167

27. Can't Smile Without Who?   173

28. I Won't Last a Day without Who?   179

29. I Don't Need to Be in Love   185

30. You Can't Hurry *Out of* Love   191

31. Someday Your Prince Will Come   197

Appendix A: What Am I Doing the Rest of Your Life?   203

Appendix B: It's Not Too Late to Turn Back Now   207

Appendix C: You'll Never Get to Heaven If . . .   213

Appendix D: You Always Hurt the One You Don't Love   219

Appendix E: You Don't Have to *Say* "I Love You"   233

Notes   243

Foreword

In this book, Lou Priolo addresses a very common human relationship problem: the problem of handling broken relationships, the problem of responding constructively to being rejected by someone for whom you have deep romantic feelings. I say this is a very common human relationship problem because of my own experience. As a young person, I personally experienced the pain of being rejected by someone for whom I had developed romantic feelings. And as a pastor, biblical counselor, and professor of biblical counseling at the Master's College, I have been called on to counsel numerous people at such a time in their lives. During the many years when I taught biblical counseling to graduate and undergraduate students, I was frequently involved in trying to help young people go through this valley time in their lives constructively. Again and again, I saw in living color the devastating effect that being rejected had on these students. As a pastor and marriage counselor for forty-five years, I have heard and seen the anguish of people when someone for whom they had deep feelings pushed them away and said, "I don't want to be with you anymore. I want out of this relationship. It's over. I want to move on."

When I am called on to counsel in such situations, in addition to the personal support I give these people in counseling sessions, I have wanted to have solid, biblically based, helpful material to put in their hands. Often, the homework I have given them has been of a rather generic sort that addresses the way a Christian can and should respond to difficult situations in his or her own life. After assigning this generic material, I have then in sessions made specific application to the particular issue the person is facing. This has often been very helpful, but I have wanted some material that was more directly and specifically related to the relationship breakup experience.

With the publication of Lou's book, all that has changed. Now, I have a great tool that is not a "one size fits all" approach to put into the hands of people. Now, I have a book that from beginning to end will provide the very kind of biblical, practical, specific help that people involved in the unwanted breakup of relationships need. Counselors who work with people who are going through this experience will find this book to be a valuable resource, as will the people who are actually experiencing the pain of broken relationships.

—Wayne Mack

Acknowledgments

This book has been in the works for years. It began with a research paper in graduate school (1985) about the impact of divorce on its casualties. Added to that are over 25 years of Bible study, 20 years of counseling those in virtually every kind of romantic heartache, and, of course, personal experience with painful relationship breakups. So there is no way I can remember even a small portion of those who have taught, helped, and encouraged me to write what you will read in these pages.

I am mindful, however, of those who, in recent days, have had a considerable impact on the *Losing That Lovin' Feeling* manuscript. They are:

Wayne Mack, for his work on responding to hurt and rejection, upon which I relied heavily in chapters 13 and 14. (Actually, Wayne has probably taught me more about counseling than anyone else.)

Amy Baker, for her help with chapter 22, which was actually the last (and most difficult) to be written.

Ingrid Davis, for her assistance with the failure material for wives.

Fern Gregory, my chief proofreader, who, by correcting my many mistakes in this and other books, has taught me more about English grammar than all my English teachers and professors combined.

June Paterson, who helped with proofreading.

Kathy Ide, who, by her editing prowess, has helped me produce a book that is more user-friendly than I could have turned out on my own.

Kim Priolo, who has supported me in dozens of selfless ways over the two years it has taken to get this book into print.

Introduction

Your Achin', Breakin' Heart

"Will this ache in my heart ever go away?"

As a professional counselor, I've been asked that question a hundred times in dozens of ways. If you are reading this book, chances are that you (or someone you love) have been asking this question, too. When a romantic relationship ends, the confluence of potentially depressing emotions can wreak havoc in the lives of those involved. This is especially true for the person who didn't want the relationship to end. But for the Christian, there is a very good answer to this oft-asked question.

Yes! Your pain will go away *in time*.

For a Christian who knows and is willing to do what the Bible says, the heartache will be healed. And the more of God's Word a person implements, the sooner the anguish will stop. If you are the one who is hurting, there are specific things you can do to ease the pain and help yourself get back to the way you were before the breakup.

Perhaps the best place to begin this process is with prayer. You can pray that God will change your heart. Your prayer may include confession of any self-centeredness or failure to love God, thanksgiving to God for His attributes, and a request that He give you a greater desire to please Him than to get over your sorrow. You can continue to pray this way until you have the assurance that the Lord has answered your prayers. You will know He has done so when you find in your heart a willingness to endure this trial for as long as it takes to produce genuine godliness in your life.

You may have already noticed that this book contains thirty-one very short chapters. After reading it through in its entirety, you may use it as a devotional guide—reading one chapter a day for a month (perhaps the chapter that best relates to whatever issue you were struggling with the day before). Depending on your unique situation and your individual strengths and weaknesses, it may take several months before you can tell that the ache in your heart is starting to diminish. Reading through this book devotionally (every day) for at least two or three months will keep before you those things you can do (as well as those things you should not do) to help you lose those lamentable "lovin' feelings" as quickly and righteously as possible.

"Righteously?"

That's right! You could battle your sorrow in sinful ways (such as constantly reminding yourself what a "turkey" your former sweetheart is),[1] but you would only end up in more misery and displease God in the process. You see, sin, which is thinking or acting independently of God, results in both temporal and eternal *misery.* You may feel pretty miserable right now, but if you don't respond biblically to the breakup, you will face another kind of misery later in life. If you do this God's way, you won't have to resort to methods that are displeasing to God. If you are a Christian, you can do it. The

Bible will show you how, the Holy Spirit will lead you, and this book will encourage you along the way.

You will learn in the pages ahead how to deal with the residual romantic feelings you may be carrying as a result of the breakup as well as other painful emotions that may be preventing you from getting on with your life. May God bless you as you respond to your trial by depending on His Spirit and His Word.

Special Instructions

If you are reading this book to help overcome romantic feelings for someone to whom you were married, or from whom you are presently separated, please turn immediately to Appendix A to receive some special instructions and guidelines for using this book.

If you are reading this book because you are attempting to overcome romantic feelings for someone with whom you've had an adulterous affair, please turn to Appendix B to receive special instructions and guidelines for using this book.

1

How Can I Mend My Broken Heart?

The backslider in heart will be filled with his own ways.
—Proverbs 14:14

Charlie's radio alarm clock went off at 6:00 A.M. The easy-listening station began playing a series of love songs. As was his habit, Charlie stayed in bed for 30 minutes or so, allowing the elevator music to slowly awaken him. But today something was different. For one thing, he couldn't help but notice how so many of the songs were about the breakup of relationships. He also noticed how many of his favorite songs had lyrics promoting selfish, feeling-oriented, idolatrous views of love.[1] The longer he lay in bed, the more depressed he became. You see, Brenda, the girl Charlie deeply loved, had dumped him the night before. She gave no reason for the breakup other than telling him that her feelings had been slowly diminishing over the past several weeks.

Charlie was devastated. "But I love her," he reminded himself as the music played. "I was going to ask her to marry me. How could she do this to me? How will I ever get along without her? How will I ever get over her?"

These mornings of misery continued for days. Sometimes Charlie stayed in bed for over an hour, tormenting himself with songs that reminded him of Brenda. Finally, he realized that the sooner he got out of bed and began putting his mind on other things, the faster his daybreak depression would subside. Small as it seemed, this was the first big step in Charlie's walk from sorrow to freedom.

We live in a world that glorifies romance more than it glorifies the God who created man and woman with the capacity to enjoy romantic relationships. This worshiping the creature rather than the Creator produces misery. Of course, not all sorrow is the result of our sin. Grief and other emotions commonly associated with a breakup, however, can become overly intense if we do not worship God as the Bible says we should.

Scripture has much to say about emotions such as grief, loneliness, rejection, anger, bitterness, guilt, and jealousy. It reveals what it takes to change these feelings, what you can do to keep them from paralyzing you, and how you can turn them around in the days ahead. The most direct way to do this is to learn how to control your thoughts and behavior.

Proverbs 14:14 warns us of the danger associated with allowing our hearts to draw back from God's resources. "The backslider in heart will be filled with his own ways." If you allow yourself to be consoled with unbiblical thoughts, you will be filled with your own ways—that is, your misery will increase. You must depend on God's solutions (and resources) to get you through this trial. Look at the counsel given in Isaiah 55:6–9.

> Seek the LORD while He may be found,
> Call upon Him while He is near.
> Let the wicked forsake his way,
> And the unrighteous man his thoughts;
> Let him return to the LORD,

And He will have mercy on him;
And to our God,
For He will abundantly pardon.

"For My thoughts are not your thoughts,
Nor are your ways My ways," says the LORD.
"For as the heavens are higher than the earth,
So are My ways higher than your ways,
And My thoughts than your thoughts."

Your ways and your *thoughts* must become God's ways and God's thoughts. In order to respond to this situation in godly ways, you need to examine your thoughts and motives so that you can be "transformed by the renewing of your mind" (Rom. 12:2).

The problem with most of us is that we listen to ourselves rather than talk to ourselves. When we go through trials, it is easier to just put our minds in neutral and listen passively to our hearts. How about you? Are you a listener or a talker? Here is a little test you can take to help answer that question.

Listed below are twenty statements representing thought patterns that are bound to produce misery in the life of someone who is experiencing the hurts of a broken relationship. After each sentence, write the number that best corresponds to how frequently the statement is true of you.

ROMANTIC THOUGHT PATTERN INVENTORY

RATING SCALE	POINTS
Never (or Hardly Ever)	5
Seldom	4
Sometimes	3
Frequently	2
Always (or Almost Always)	1

1. When thinking about the future, I imagine how miserable I will be without the companionship of my ex[2] rather than imagining how God is going to cause all things to work together for my good. _____

2. I allow myself to fantasize about things I know will probably never materialize. _____

3. I spend more time thinking about my ex than about God, His Word, or delights of eternal significance. _____

4. I dwell on or exaggerate the shortcomings of my ex to remind myself of how glad I should be that I am rid of him. _____

5. I give in to depression rather than trying to fight it. _____

6. I put the worst possible interpretation on the actions of my ex. _____

7. I struggle with vain regrets (looking at the past in such a way that it keeps me from living biblically, responsively, and productively in the present). _____

8. I wish I were someone else or someplace else. _____

9. I feel guilty because I know I've not acknowledged or sought forgiveness for my own sins that contributed to the breakdown of the relationship. _____

I have thought or said the following:

10. "It will be a long time before I can forgive my ex." _____

11. "I hope someday somebody does to her what she did to me." _____

12. "I can't adjust to being single again." _____

13. "I'm a total failure." _____

14. "The loneliness is more than I can stand." _____

15. "The embarrassment is more than I can stand." _____

16. "The rejection is more than I can stand." _____

17. "All men (women) are alike." _____

18. "I can't believe God is doing this to me again!" _____

19. "Life isn't worth living anymore." _____

20. "I'll never be able to face my family and friends again." _____

Total Points _____

How did you do? The closer your score is to 100, the more you are thinking biblically about the breakup of your relationship. Let me suggest that you take this test every thirty days over the next few months to monitor your progress. If you scored lower than 75, you may want to read one chapter of this book daily for several months until you can raise your score to at least that level.

So what are you doing with your thought life these days? Are you spending too much time allowing your mind to dwell on the past or worrying about the future rather than focusing your thoughts on what God has given you to do today? Are you listening to the lies that your flesh tempts you to believe, or do you speak the truth in your heart, knowing that God has given you all the resources necessary to "fall out of love" biblically? If you do the former, you are in for extended periods of unnecessary heartache. If you do the latter, you can be transformed by the renewing of your mind.

You will find in the pages ahead practical biblical insight that will not only help you improve your test score but, more importantly, draw you closer to God as you deal with the hurt of your broken relationship.

2

Have You Tossed Those Lovin' Feelings?

But the fruit of the Spirit is love, joy, peace, longsuffering, kindness, goodness, faithfulness, gentleness, self-control.
—Galatians 5:22–23

Before we proceed any further, it might be helpful if we take a crash course in the theology of emotions in order to help you better understand what part feelings play in life and to what extent we should trust and follow them.

Have you ever wondered why you can't just turn off your feelings the way you turn off the kitchen light? Wouldn't it be nice if, after you got tired of a particular feeling (such as anxiety, loneliness, depression, grief, or guilt), you could simply hit some kind of button and turn it off? Actually, it wouldn't be such a good thing if you could turn off your feelings at will. As we will see, emotions (even painful ones) play an important part in our lives. Thankfully, God didn't make our emotions so that they could be easily controlled. You can't get at them or control them directly. You can access them only indirectly—through your thoughts and actions.

"I'm not sure I agree with you. I'm not really comfortable with the thought that they're as indirectly accessible for modification as you seem to believe."

I understand your apprehension with this suggestion. But please allow me to persuade you by giving you a chance to directly alter your feelings right now. I'd like you to try to emote and then stop emoting on command. Let's see how long it takes you to turn your feelings on and off. Are you ready? Good. Sit up straight in your chair, take a couple of deep breaths, and we'll begin the experiment.

On the count of three, I want you to become frightened. One, two, three: *Be afraid*. That's right—try to work up a colossal measure of stark, abject fear. Come on, you can do it! Concentrate! Reach down into the depths of your being and grunt it out.

It didn't work, did it?

"No, I guess it didn't."

Most people can't work up a good fright without spending a considerable amount of time *thinking* about the danger of a potentially hazardous circumstance. If you're not currently facing such a hazard, you would have to imagine one to become frightened. Of course, if you could immediately place yourself in real danger by some *action*, you might then more easily become frightened. You see, your emotions are directly connected to your thoughts and actions. To change your feelings, you usually have to change your thoughts and your ways.

Now let's try something else. Let's see if you can *stop* emoting on command. Please sit up straight in your chair again, take another deep breath, and on the count of three we'll begin. One, two, three: *fall out of love!* Try to stop loving that person you've been in love with for so long. Come on, focus really hard. Reach down into the depths of your heart and turn off the flow of those sentimental emotions that have been causing you so much pain of late. You do want them to go away, don't you? Well, then, "just say no" to those hurtful feelings. Stop tormenting yourself with those warm, fuzzy memories from the past. Stop yearning for his/her companionship. Stop feeling so hurt and rejected. Turn off those passion switches.

Well, how did you do? That didn't work either, did it?

"You knew it wouldn't!"

You might succeed in temporarily getting your ex out of your mind by thinking about something or someone else. But even that would have proved my point: you have to change your thinking to change your feelings. I trust that you're now convinced (or at least a little more open to the likelihood) that people can't change their affections directly. We can't instantly and permanently turn our feelings on and off at will, but we can gradually turn them around.

"All right, I guess you made your point, but what do you mean about turning feelings around? And how can I do that?"

With the Holy Spirit's enabling power, you can develop self-control—a magnificent piece of the Spirit's fruit described by the apostle Paul in Galatians 5:23. By learning how to control those things that control your emotions, you can turn them around. In other words, by learning how to exercise self-control over your thoughts and actions, you can ultimately train your emotions to go in a new direction—a direction that works with you to accomplish your goals rather than against you.

Self-control is the ability to consistently make wise decisions and fulfill responsibilities on the basis of God's Word rather than on the basis of one's feelings. Self-control has to do with *not* giving in to your feelings. The greatest hindrance to developing self-discipline is your feelings. The greatest enemy of self-control is your feelings. People who are self-disciplined do (and think about) what the Bible says whether or not they feel like it. People without self-control do what they feel like doing, regardless of what the Bible says.

Self-control is largely a matter of learning how to go against your feelings. It's about becoming less of a feeling-oriented person and more of an obedience-oriented person.

In the process of getting over a broken relationship, self-control involves doing and thinking what the Bible says you should even though you feel otherwise. It involves thinking about your ex in God-honoring ways though you may *feel* like thinking the opposite.

That may sound like hypocrisy, but it is not hypocritical to feel one thing and do something else any more than it's hypocritical to do something loving for someone even when you don't feel like doing it. (John 3:16 doesn't say, "For God so loved the world that He felt warm and fuzzy inside.") It would be hypocrisy for you to *profess* one thing and do another. If you said, "I'm really glad this relationship is over" when you weren't, or "Changing the way I think about my ex was easy" when it wasn't, that would be hypocrisy. But to struggle against your flesh (Matt. 26:41; Rom. 8:5, 13; Gal. 5:17) in obedience to God's Word so that your thoughts and ways may glorify Him is not hypocrisy.

Another definition of this important character quality[1] has to do with managing one's emotions. Self-control is the ability to rule one's own spirit through the power of the Holy Spirit. "He who is slow to anger is better than the mighty, and he who rules his spirit than he who takes a city" (Prov. 16:32). Solomon says that if you can control your emotions, you are, in God's eyes, greater than a famous military leader such as General Patton or General Schwarzkopf.

Solomon also warned us of the dangers associated with not being self-disciplined. "Whoever has no rule over his own spirit is like a city broken down, without walls" (Prov. 25:28). A city without walls is vulnerable to all kinds of peril. If you allow the unpleasant feelings generated by your broken relationship to get the better of you, they will make you vulnerable to such dangers as neglect of family, friends, church, school, and work activities, the development of unhealthy future relationships, self-pity, guilt, and even difficulty trusting God in the future. So to be hooked on a feeling can be as dangerous as being hooked on drugs.

To change your feelings *in the long run*, you must learn to develop self-control. But *in the short run*, you must not let your feelings hinder the Spirit as He helps you develop self-control. By God's grace, you can say no to your feelings when your feelings are tempting you to disobey God.

3

How Do Fools "Fall in Love"?

He who trusts in his own heart is a fool, but whoever walks wisely will be delivered. —Proverbs 28:26

People "fall in love"[1] because they want to. When you "fell in love," you were not struck with some external force such as Cupid's arrow. Neither were you dazzled by some external influence such as Love Potion #9. The romantic feelings you enjoyed, which you are now struggling to abate, are of your own making. They were created in your own heart. They, like your other feelings, are largely the result of your thoughts and ways. You "fell in love" with your ex as a result of what you *did to, for,* and *with* him and as a result of what you *told yourself* about her. You created those romantic feelings, and by God's grace, you can make them go away.

Think for a moment about what you did when the two of you were first courting. Didn't you spend lots of time doing fun things together? Didn't you invest hour after hour revealing your heart to him and listening to her reveal her heart to you? Didn't you spend time, money, and effort doing things for him—even while you were apart? Didn't you think often about all those wonderful qualities in your sweetheart that you admired? In fact, wasn't the majority of your spare time (and even some "not so spare" time) consumed with musings about how wonderful your relationship with your special friend was? Wasn't your imagination often engaged in anticipation of spending lots of time with this person?

The totality of these mental, emotional, and behavioral investments generated those feelings that our culture equates with "falling in love." Consequently, the more you did *to*, *with*, and *for* the other person, and the more time you spent thinking such loving thoughts about him, the greater the potential you had to develop feelings of love. And if your sweetheart was doing the same kinds of loving things to, with, and for you, the feelings became even more intense. Moreover, if your relationship was relatively free of conflict and your partner was putting her "best foot forward," you may not have had enough information to balance those feelings of love with wisdom.

But is love a feeling?

Biblical love is not primarily a feeling. Love is fundamentally a *verb*. First Corinthians Chapter 13, even in the eyes of many pagans, is unsurpassed for its accuracy and literary genius.

"Love is patient, love is kind, and is not jealous; love does not brag and is not arrogant, does not act unbecomingly; it does not seek its own, is not provoked, does not take into account a wrong suffered, does not rejoice in unrighteousness, but rejoices with the truth; bears all things, believes all things, hopes all things, endures all things" (1 Cor. 13:4–7 NASV).[2]

Now let me break this passage down into its component parts of speech so that you can see for yourself what I'm talking about. Love is patient: "is patient" in the original Greek New Testament is one participle: it is *verbal* in nature. Love is kind: "is kind" is likewise a *verbal* participle. "Is not jealous": also a *verb*. And so it is for all the rest:

Love does not brag and	Verb
Is not arrogant,	Verb
Does not act unbecomingly;	Verb
It does not seek its own,	Verb
Is not provoked,	Verb
Does not take into account a wrong suffered,	Verb
Does not rejoice in unrighteousness,	Verb
But rejoices with the truth;	Verb
Bears all things,	Verb
Believes all things,	Verb
Hopes all things,	Verb
Endures all things.	Verb

When God described *love*, He used *verbs* because love is something you *do* much more than something you *feel*. It involves *motion* much more than it does *emotion*.

Although love *involves* our emotions, it is not primarily *an* emotion. The feelings associated with "falling in love" may be the result of a person implementing 1 Corinthians 13 in a variety of thoughtful and practical ways, or they may be the result of thinking and doing some very selfish (unloving) things. In other words, the feelings of "falling in love" may not be feelings of love at all—they may be feelings of selfishness.

"So how can I tell the difference between the two?"

You can't really discern the difference by trying to evaluate your feelings. You must look at the content of your thoughts and actions. If your feelings are the result of those things the Bible calls love, you really do love the other person. If, however, you have not loved the other person according to 1 Corinthians 13, you should be very suspicious of your feelings.

Wisdom is the antidote to the folly of trusting in and following your feelings. "He who trusts in his own heart is a fool, but whoever walks wisely will be delivered" (Prov. 28:26). The heart, according to Jeremiah 17:9, "is deceitful above all things, and desperately wicked; who can know it?" Rather than simply trusting your feelings to be the barometer of your love, why not evaluate the degree to which you love the other person by the infallible, objective standard of God's Word?

In chapter 5, we'll take a closer look at other elements of biblical love.

Since you "fell in love" by ordering your thoughts and actions in certain ways, you can "fall out of love" by ordering your thoughts and actions in different ways. Are you willing to forsake your own way of responding to your ex so that you may glorify God in all you do? Are you willing to learn how to mend your ways and restructure your thought patterns so that in time the intensity of your passions will subside? If so, why not make that commitment to the Lord today, thanking Him for the enabling power of His Spirit and His Word, and asking Him for the wisdom and the grace to apply what you will be studying in the pages that follow.

4

Only *Love* Can Break a Heart?

I now rejoice, not that you were made sorrowful, but that you were made sorrowful to the point of repentance; for you were made sorrowful according to the will of God. . . . For the sorrow that is according to the will of God produces a repentance without regret, leading to salvation, but the sorrow of the world produces death.
—*2 Corinthians 7:9–10 NASB*

Our understanding of the theology of feelings would not be complete without comprehending the place of unpleasant emotions in the life of a believer. God made each of us with the capacity to experience and enjoy a variety of emotions. Every emotion God created has power for good as well as potential for evil.

"What about emotions like hate or jealousy—can they ever be good?"

Sure! In fact, as Christians, we are commanded to hate. "You who love the LORD, *hate* evil!" (Ps. 97:10). Listen to Solomon talk about hate: "The fear of the LORD is to hate evil; pride and arrogance and the evil way and the perverse mouth I hate" (Prov. 8:13).

Then there is jealousy (which we will look at more closely in chapter 24). Paul had a righteous jealousy for the Corinthians. "For I am jealous for you with godly jealousy. For I have betrothed you to one husband, that I may present you as a chaste virgin to Christ" (2 Cor. 11:2). Fundamentally, jealousy is fear—the fear of displacement. Paul was jealous with a *godly* jealousy. He was *afraid* that His spiritual daughter (the Corinthians), whom he had promised in marriage to Christ, might not remain a virgin until the time of the wedding. He wanted to present his daughter to her Husband as a pure virgin. His concern was *not* that of a *selfish* father who was fearful of losing his *dowry*, but that of a *loving* father who was concerned for the spiritual wellbeing of his children, whom he dearly loved.

God has placed in the human body the capacity to experience physical pain. He also put in the spirit of man the capability of triggering painful emotions such as anxiety, fear, bitterness, loneliness, guilt, depression, rejection, and despair. There is a positive function for these "negative" emotions.[1]

Most of us would never seek the help of a physician unless we were in some kind of physical pain. Such pain, therefore, can be a good thing because it lets us know something is wrong. Similarly, most of us would never seek the help of a counselor unless we were in some kind of emotional distress. These painful emotions can be a good thing because they let us know something is wrong. This kind of pain should be viewed as a symptom. It's God's way of letting us know that something may be wrong in our lives.

Imagine lying in bed at 3:30 A.M. when all of a sudden your smoke detector startles you from a sound sleep. Can you believe the nerve of that smoke detector to wake you up out of a sound sleep by piercing the night with its cacophonous 103-decibel distress signal! How are you ever going to get back to sleep with that continuous piercing alarm screaming in your ears?

"We'll just see about that!" you say to yourself as you jam your fingers into your ears, pull the pillow over your head, and try to fall back to sleep.

After ten minutes of torment, you unplug your ears and begin to grope around under your bed for the nearest shoe. Then you throw off the covers, jump out of bed, stomp off toward the smoke detector with boot in hand, and commence to smash the smoke detector to smithereens.

"That's absurd!"

Why is that absurd?

"Because the real problem is not with the smoke detector. It's with the fire that set off the smoke detector!"

Exactly! It is foolish to smash the smoke detector when it's doing what it was designed to do and is working only too well. Yet this is often the way people try to deal with their emotions. They ignore them, hoping the pain will go away. Or they turn to alcohol, run to the psychiatrist's office in the hope of persuading him to prescribe some pill (or perhaps something more radical like electroshock therapy), or do whatever else it takes to make the pain go away. In their desperation, they never stop to consider that the real problem may not be with their emotions at all, but with some other fire in their lives.

"Are you saying that all painful emotions are the result of our own sin?"

Certainly not. All misery, including most pain, is the result of sin, but as I've already pointed out, not all pain is the result of *our own* sin. Christ was without sin; yet He was "a Man of sorrows and acquainted with grief" (Isa. 53:3; cf. Matt. 26:38). He said, "Blessed are those who mourn" (Matt. 5:4). He could "sympathize with our weaknesses" (Heb. 4:15). He became angry

(Mark 3:5) and indignant[2] (Mark 10:14). He wept over the death of His friend (John 11:34–35) and the city of Jerusalem (Luke 19:41).

It is clear that not all potentially distressing emotions are the result of personal sin. They may simply be the normal result of adjusting to new and stressful circumstances that God has brought into our lives. They may be attributed to physiological causes such as illness or fatigue. Factors such as these cannot be ignored when considering potential causes of distressing emotions. Often our emotions are the result of a combination of factors.

Since Jesus Christ was perfect and could not sin, He never experienced any emotion that was the result of His own sin—He never needed an emotional smoke detector to alert Him to personal wrongdoing. You and I, however, often experience feelings that warn us about sin in our lives.

The chart below is a page of an owner's manual that explains how to use your "emotion detection device." The chart can be used in much the same way as the troubleshooting guide that comes with your automobile, computer, camera, wristwatch, or microwave oven. The first column describes the siren, or painful emotion you may be experiencing. The second column alerts you to what might be causing the alarm to go off. Later, I will explain what sets off these sirens (as well as how to put out their corresponding fires).

EMOTIONAL TROUBLESHOOTING GUIDE

Sinful Anger	☐ I may not have submitted my desires to God. ☐ I may be guilty of idolatry (loving something more than God).
Fear	☐ I may not love God as I should. ☐ I may not love my neighbor as I should.

Loneliness	☐ I may be expecting others to meet my needs rather than God.
Anxiety	☐ I may not trust God as I should. ☐ I may have a temporal value system. ☐ I may be guilty of idolatry (loving something more than God).
Depression	☐ I may not have properly dealt with guilt. ☐ I may not have forgiven someone who hurt me. ☐ I may not have been fulfilling my biblical responsibilities.
Excessive Sorrow	☐ I may love that which I have lost more than I love God. ☐ I may not be focusing my thoughts on the right things.
Jealousy	☐ I may be looking to someone other than God to meet my needs. ☐ I may have a temporal value system.
Bitterness	☐ I may not have forgiven someone who hurt me. ☐ I may not have rightly confronted my offender.

Since the suggestions I've listed are far from exhaustive, you may wonder how to figure out which option(s) applies to you. That's where the Bible comes in. "The word of God . . . is a discerner of the thoughts and intents of the heart" (Heb. 4:12). Prayerfully use the Scriptures to discern the cause of the problem—not in words taught by human wisdom but by the Spirit, expressing spiritual truths in spiritual words (cf. 1 Cor. 2:13). This book can get you off to a good start, but if you want to use the Bible as God intended, become a better student of the Word. You may even want to find someone to teach you.

In 2 Corinthians 7:9–10, the apostle Paul knew that his letter to the Corinthians was going to cause some of them great sorrow. Yet he wrote it, hoping that the Spirit's convicting ministry would use it to motivate them to repent. His letter was a wake-up call (a warning siren, if you please) designed to produce godly sorrow.

"You mean he purposely did something that he knew would cause pain?"

Sure. It may surprise you to learn that it's not necessarily a sin to hurt someone's feelings. It is sometimes necessary in the process of speaking the truth in love to say something that produces a small measure of temporary discomfort in those to whom we minister in order to motivate them to repent. Similarly, God may allow us to experience a variety of distressing emotions to motivate us to change our thoughts and ways.

That is the positive side of negative emotions. They often function as God's "smoke detectors" to let us know there are fires in our lives. Our smoke detectors will not go off for good until the fires are put out.

The distressing emotions that you are currently experiencing as a result of your broken relationship may be generated by several sources. Remember, the long-term solution is not to smash the smoke detector. The solution is to find out what is making the smoke detector go off and to put out the fire.

5

Can't I Stop Loving You?

You have heard that it was said, "You shall love your neighbor and hate your enemy." But I say to you, love your enemies, bless those who curse you, do good to those who hate you, and pray for those who spitefully use you and persecute you, that you may be sons of your Father in heaven; for He makes His sun rise on the evil and on the good, and sends rain on the just and on the unjust.
—Matthew 5:43–45

A re you ready for a real shocker? If you want to "fall out of love" with your ex, you're going to have to love him even more than you did before!

"Now, wait a minute! I thought you said that if I wanted to 'fall out of love,' I would have to *stop* doing those loving things I did *to, for,* and *with* my ex. You know—all those things I used to do and think that you claimed produced these feelings you're trying to help me change! Which is it? Do I love my ex more or less?"

Technically you will have to love him more—not with more intensity, but with more specificity. Remember, love is a verb more than a noun. It is *motion* more than *emotion*. Since Christians are commanded to love not only our neighbors but also our enemies (Matt. 5:44), "falling out of love" is not simply a matter of no longer doing loving things to, for, and with your ex. It's a matter of loving in new and different ways—ways that will not generate more romantic feelings but will actually help them subside. In other words, rather than loving up close and personal, you will have to learn how to love from a distance. Rather than thinking in terms of *external* manifestations of love (which may have been your practice by virtue of all the time the two of you spent in each other's presence and communicating with each other), you'll have to think in terms of *internal* ones (since the two of you will no longer be spending time together or communicating nearly as much as you did in the past).

Manifestations of Love

"What do you mean by external and internal manifestations of love?"

External manifestations of love are those related to your words and actions. Internal manifestations of love are those relating to your thoughts and motives. Look again at the description of biblical love.

> Love is patient.
> Love is kind.
> Love is not jealous.
> Love does not brag.
> Love is not arrogant.
> Love does not act unbecomingly.
> Love does not seek its own.
> Love is not provoked.
> Love does not take into account a wrong suffered.

Love does not rejoice in unrighteousness.
Love rejoices with the truth.
Love bears all things.
Love believes all things.
Love hopes all things.
Love endures all things. (see 1 Cor. 13:4–7 NASB)

Each of these elements describes positive and negative[1] aspects of what love looks like. For the most part, they are observable external behaviors. But they describe something internal—an attitude of the heart that involves giving oneself unselfishly for the benefit of another.

Up to this point, you've had opportunity to demonstrate each of these elements of love to your ex in tangible ways. Now you must learn how to love this person in absentia. You should drastically limit the amount of time you spend thinking about her. But when you do, be careful to control the way you think about her, so that you do not allow yourself to develop unloving attitudes (such as bitterness, jealousy, or contempt) that could result in unloving words or actions. If you change the content of your thought patterns, your love will take on a new form.

Consider for a moment God's love for us. Isn't His love sometimes manifested in forms that appear contradictory to each other? For example, sometimes His love is demonstrated when He does something special in answer to prayer that is "exceedingly abundantly above all that we ask or think" (Eph. 3:20). At other times, His love takes on the form of a divine spanking: "For whom the LORD loves He chastens" (Heb. 12:6, quoting Prov. 3:12). These two manifestations of love may appear dissimilar on the surface, but when viewed from a biblical perspective, they are simply different forms of the same thing.

So it is with you. You may have to reexamine 1 Corinthians 13:4–7 in light of learning to love your ex in different ways. For instance, instead of fulfilling the "love is patient" clause by restraining your anger[2] when he keeps you waiting too long, you may now have to be patient by restraining your anger over the way in which the relationship ended, over the fact that your ex has not yet acknowledged how he has hurt you, or over the way he may be misrepresenting to others the exact nature of the breakup.

As for the "love is kind" component, rather than simply showing kindness directly to your sweetheart in word and deed when she is ill or irritable, you may now have to do so by saying kind things to others about her. You will need to be extra careful to avoid all elements of cruelty and harshness (two antitheses of kindness). And you will have to do so not only in any direct dealings with your ex, but also in your communications about her to others.

Let's jump down the list a bit to "love does not act unbecomingly."[3] This is the fourth in a list of eight consecutive negative aspects of love, each of which is intended to draw attention to its opposite. To act unbecomingly is to act in an ugly way or to do something that will later cause shame. When you were actively involved in a relationship, you were careful not to say or do ugly, shameful things. You made a conscious effort to be honorable in all your dealings with him. You were polite, attentive, courteous, and considerate, used good table manners, and were thoughtful of his needs and desires. You avoided crude remarks, foul language, vitriolic comments, pejorative utterances, selfish decisions, gossip, and slander.

At this juncture, you may not have as many opportunities to practice the positive side of this element. (Although when you are in the presence of your ex, you should continue to do constructive things as much as possible.) But you will have plenty of opportunity to practice not doing and saying negative, destructive things to or about your ex. Moreover, you will almost certainly be more tempted to do and say destructive things now that the relationship is over as you discuss the breakup with those who love you. Perhaps you've already done some unseemly things since the breakup. Confess those to the Lord (if you haven't already done so). Ask His forgiveness as well as the forgiveness of those to whom you've said unloving things. From now on, as much as possible, commit yourself to doing and saying honorable things in reference to your ex.

Of all the ways you may "love" your ex from this point forward, perhaps the two most important are to "think no evil" and to "believe all things" about her. These elements are different sides (negative and positive) of the same coin. They have to do with the moment-by-moment decisions you make concerning the manner in which you think about the object of your love. To "think no evil" means not keeping a running list of wrongs that the other person has committed against you. It's the result of overlooking someone's debt, of no longer holding a person's transgressions against him. Such "forgetfulness" is not forgetting in the sense of having amnesia, but in the refusing to call to mind that which has been forgiven.

To "believe all things" is to put the best possible spin on a person's behavior. Say your ex does something that could be viewed in ten different ways, nine of which are bad. Love will reject the nine and accept the one. In the absence of hard evidence to the contrary, love will go out of its way (investing time, effort, and thought) to imagine a good interpretation of the matter before seriously considering a bad one. Love doesn't slam the gavel down on the judicial bench of its mind, declaring a person guilty, without looking seriously at all the evidence (which, by the way, is often not readily available). Can you love your ex in this way? You can if you are a Christian who has been forgiven of your sins and has had the love of God poured into your heart (Rom. 5:5).

At the back of this book, Appendix E has a worksheet that contains a partially completed list of specific ways a person may demonstrate all fourteen elements of 1 Corinthians 13 love to a former boyfriend, girlfriend, fiancé, fiancée, or spouse. It is partial because it was designed to be personalized by you according to your own particular set of circumstances. Why not take a moment right now and begin making your own list of specific ways you can love your ex in absentia?

6

Love Isn't Blue

Why are you cast down, O my soul? And why are you disquieted within me? Hope in God; for I shall yet praise Him, the help of my countenance and my God.
—Psalm 43:5

Depression is probably the most common emotion with which people who have gone through breakups seem to struggle. There are physiological as well as nonorganic causes for this condition. In this chapter, I'll identify three of the most common nonorganic causes. As we move through the book, you'll encounter additional ways of avoiding and defeating them.

The most basic cause of spiritual depression is living out of harmony with Scripture. But to simply call something "sin" without identifying its exact biblical designation does not help us effectively treat the problem. Just as a physician can prescribe a specific antibiotic once he's identified the exact strain of bacteria causing an infection, I hope to help you arrive at a more accurate diagnosis of (and remedy for) any functional (nonmedical) depression you may be experiencing.

Unrepentant Sin

The first category of sin that causes depression is the *unrepentant sin*. By this, I mean any sin about which you feel guilty.[1] Someone has likened guilt to the physical exhaustion that occurs when an individual exercises too long. Overexerting oneself during physical exercise will ultimately result in a temporary depletion of strength and vigor. Running around the track too many times, for example, will eventually sap a person of his physical energy and cause him to become physically exhausted. Similarly, living day in and day out with guilt over sin that has not been confessed expends a certain amount of emotional energy. It saps your emotional strength and causes you to become emotionally exhausted (i.e., depressed). God didn't design guilt to be something that His people were to live with for long periods of time. His intention is for us to confess our sin and forsake it. In so doing, we experience both forgiveness through Christ and sanctification through the Holy Spirit.[2] These two provisions eliminate guilt. Appropriating God's forgiveness removes the guilt of our past sins.[3] Cooperating with Him in the sanctification process removes the guilt we sometimes experience as a result of the knowledge that we are bound by a particular sinful habit and will therefore likely commit the same sin tomorrow.

Certain sins, in addition to producing guilt, have other side effects that will sap emotional energy and produce depression. The greatest of these is bitterness. Bitterness (or resentment) is the result of an unwillingness to forgive those who have sinned against you. It requires emotional energy to maintain a grudge. Resentment, like guilt, will deplete your energy if allowed to reside in your heart too long. Remember, these feelings are God's "smoke detectors" designed to call attention to a particular fire issue in our lives. They can't be ignored without long-term damage to the body and soul. Other sins that drain our emotional energy (above and beyond any guilt they might cause) include

46

anxiety, unrighteous anger, selfish fear, and jealousy. We will examine all of these in the pages ahead.

Mental-Attitude Sin

The next classification of nonorganic depression has to do with mental-attitude sins. Perhaps the best way to categorize them is as *wrong values*. When people do not view life as God does, misery results. As Christians, we must train ourselves to think as the Bible says we should think, to love the things He loves, to hate the things He hates, to long for the things He wants us to long for, and to not want the things He doesn't want us to have. In other words, for us to be happy (the antithesis of being depressed), we must think and be motivated biblically.

Depression often occurs when people have sinful thoughts and motives. They think thoughts that God says they shouldn't think. They fear the things He doesn't want them to fear. They do not fear Him as much as He wants them to fear Him. They worry about things about which He says not to worry. They interpret circumstances in ways that do not reflect God's sovereignty, love, or goodness. They are unthankful for His blessings. They want what God says they can't have. They love what God says they shouldn't love (or love too much what God has given them to enjoy in moderation). They value too highly things God doesn't value highly (if at all). They don't value the things He values most. Is it really any wonder that so many people in our society are depressed?

Mishandling Difficult Situations

The third cause of spiritual depression is *mishandling difficult situations*. God leads His children into a variety of trials designed to perfect their character and ultimately result in their happiness. But when they do not avail themselves of the resources He has given them to respond biblically to a trial, they can grow discouraged, bitter, guilt-ridden, anxious, and fearful. All of these can lead to depression. How we respond to the difficult circumstances God brings into our lives determines the extent to which we will be depressed about those circumstances.

Just this morning, I learned that yesterday a friend of mine, after discovering that her husband had made a series of foolish decisions, fractured her arm (the result of punching him in the head). The interesting thing is that just a few hours before this episode, I explained to her that if she would forgive her hardheaded husband, she would minimize the effects of her husband's sin on her entire family. I also made it clear that if she didn't respond biblically to her difficult situation, she would maximize her misery. Now she carries with her a monument of her sinful response in the form of a cast that she'll be wearing for the next six to eight weeks. I intend to encourage her to use that cast as a daily reminder of what happens when we don't respond biblically to the trials God sends our way.[4]

How you respond to a breakup will have a direct bearing on how depressed you will be in the weeks and months ahead. Will you make every effort to view the breakup as from the Lord,[5] depending on Him to teach you to think and behave in a God-honoring way? Or will you continue interpreting the breakup selfishly, responding sinfully in thought, word, and deed?

Perhaps it's time for you to ask yourself, as the psalmist did, "Why are you cast down, O my soul? And why are you disquieted within me?" This question was meant to be asked as a self-rebuke. "In light of God's wonderful provisions, what right do you have to be despairing and troubled?" But I'm suggesting, if you're battling depression, that you ask yourself the question more diagnostically as you read through the remaining chapters of this book. "Why (for what reasons) am I discouraged and depressed?"

"I can do that! But I have a question about this passage we're discussing. I know that the Lord is 'my God,' but how is He 'the help of my countenance'?"

These sins, as well as many others, can also affect the way we look. The Bible identifies some of the sins that affect our countenance: cf. Gen. 4:5–6; 31:2, 5; Ps. 10:4; Isa. 3:9; Ezek. 27:35; Dan. 5:6, 9–10). God is the only One who can remove from our lives those sins that mar our countenance.[6]

Cheer up. Take hope in God. He is the help of your countenance. If you respond biblically to this trial, you shall yet praise Him.

7

Why Are You Lonesome Tonight?

Indeed the hour is coming, yes, has now come, that you will be scattered, each to his own, and will leave Me alone. And yet I am not alone, because the Father is with Me. These things I have spoken to you, that in Me you may have peace. In the world you will have tribulation; but be of good cheer, I have overcome the world.
—John 16:32–33

God designed most of us so that we would be lonely without the company of a lifelong companion. In the second chapter of Genesis (v. 18), He said, "It is not good for the man to be alone. I will make a helper suitable for him" (NIV).

But here you are, alone again, longing for a permanent solution to your lack of companionship. "How lonely will I be without a companion?" you wonder. "Am I doomed to a life of loneliness?" Only the sovereign Creator and Sustainer of the universe knows

51

what your future holds. Your job is to trust Him to meet any need for companionship you might have in His own way and His own time. For most of us, it is a good thing to be married. As Solomon said in Proverbs 18:22, "He who finds a wife finds a good thing, and obtains favor from the LORD." When we are unmarried, our primary goal must not be to get married but rather to please God. We have the assurance that "no good thing will He withhold from those who walk uprightly" (Ps. 84:11).

What Is Loneliness?

So what is loneliness? Many view loneliness simply as not having the company of others. But loneliness can also be the result of not being in fellowship with God. When I speak of "fellowship with God," I do not mean a mystical intimacy whereby the Holy Spirit whispers in your ear words of comfort and assurance.[1] Rather, I'm referring to the assurance that comes from confessing and forsaking all known sin and the sense of closeness to God that comes from having a clean conscience and drawing near to Him through Bible study and prayer. Such fellowship doesn't necessarily displace a person's desire for marriage or companionship but will provide a sense of contentment that will blunt the edge of loneliness. "Let your conduct be without covetousness; be content with such things as you have. For He Himself has said, 'I will never leave you nor forsake you'" (Heb. 13:5, quoting Josh. 1:5).

In chapter 2, I pointed out that in order to change your feelings, you have to change your thoughts and your actions. May I suggest that loneliness is also more of a state of mind than it is a feeling. The way you *think* about being alone will affect the way you *feel* about it. If you believe that you must always have another human being at your side to avoid being lonely, you are likely to be a very lonely person.

There will probably be times when you will feel lonely even in a room filled with people. On the other hand, if you arm yourself with the biblical mind-set that loneliness is primarily the result of not being in fellowship with God,[2] you may find that you feel less lonely even when you are alone.

Jesus knew He was going to be forsaken by His disciples (John 16:32), but He also knew He wasn't really alone because the Father was with Him. He viewed being *left alone* and *being alone* as two different things. His mind-set was not "I will necessarily be lonely as a result of being left alone," but seems rather to have been "as long as the Father is with Me, I will not be lonely even though all forsake Me." He knew that God's presence and provision were more than adequate to make up for the loss of all other company.

In chapter 4, I suggested that loneliness is sometimes the result of expecting others to meet our needs, rather than God. When loneliness is the result of such unbiblical thinking, it reveals an idolatrous heart. The Bible, in at least two different places, equates covetousness with idolatry. You grew accustomed to having your ex keep you company. While it is not wrong to experience such companionship, especially in the bond of matrimony, sometimes people substitute the company of companions for God's company. Have you been guilty of displacing God with your ex? Could loneliness be God's way of letting you know that you have been guilty of idolatry?

"Well, maybe to some extent—but how can God, who is a Spirit, meet my desire for companionship?"

God is able to minister to us in our loneliness *through other people*. But He also ministers to us in a more immediate, direct, and personal way: *through prayer and the Word*.

I once heard a story about a family of three whose car broke down late one night in front of an old farmhouse during a severe thunderstorm. The father ran up to the door of the house and asked the farmer if he would be willing to put his family up for the night. The farmer agreed to let them stay but explained that the extra bedroom contained only a set of bunk beds. The man thanked the farmer and quickly brought his wife and daughter into the house.

As they settled into bed, the little girl was given the top bunk; the man and his wife took the bottom one. When the lights were turned off, the thunder and lightning grew worse. The little girl became frightened and asked her father for some comfort.

"Daddy, I'm afraid!"

"Now, honey, there is nothing to be afraid of . . . Jesus is up there with you," came the voice from below.

After a few moments, as the storm continued to rage, the little girl tried again.

"Daddy, I'm afraid!"

"Sweetheart, I told you there is nothing to worry about. The Lord is with you up there."

Suddenly a clap of thunder exploded very close to the farmhouse. The little girl immediately cried out, "Daddy, can you please come up here with God and let me come down there with Mommy?"

For some, the thought of God's being able to comfort us in our loneliness is about as appealing as the thought of God's comforting that little girl in the thunderstorm was to her. "Thanks for the offer, but I'd rather be ministered to by someone with flesh and blood."

The Holy Spirit will comfort us in our loneliness as He will in any other trouble (2 Cor. 1:3–5). But He will do so in proportion to the time we spend in Bible study (reading, memorizing, and meditating on Scripture) and prayer. The Spirit works in conjunction with the Word. You must give the Spirit His most powerful weapon if you want Him to assist you in your trials. Take "the sword of the Spirit, which is the word[3] of God" (Eph. 6:17), so that He will have what He needs to comfort you most effectively.

How much time did you spend in the presence of your ex cultivating a relationship when you were together? The time you spent communicating with your ex helped diminish your loneliness. How does the time you spent in the presence of your ex compare with the time you now spend in prayer and the Word? What do you suppose would happen to your loneliness if you spent even half as much time with God as you did with your ex? What if you invested half as much time meditating on Scripture as you did being mentally preoccupied with him?

Loneliness can also be the result of having a defective relationship with God. Sometimes people are lonely because they have never been saved from their sin. (They have never truly put their trust in Christ's substitutionary death on the cross.) Consequently, they have not been indwelt by the Holy Spirit and do not have His abiding presence in their lives. If you have any doubts as to whether you have been born again, please take a moment right now to read Appendix C.

One Final Point

A little loneliness is more tolerable than you may realize. Be careful to guard your heart from magnifying what is a *tolerable* trial into one that is an *unbearable* one. You will probably have to live with some amount of loneliness as long as you are "absent from the Lord" (2 Cor. 5:6).

Living in a sin-cursed world precludes ultimate happiness in this life. We live not for this world but for the next. Until the Lord returns, sin, suffering, sickness, and Satan will be with us. Loneliness can be a good thing, not only because it lets us know that it's time to draw closer to God, but also because it makes us long to be with Christ for all eternity.

8

There Goes My Security Thing

Do not lay up for yourselves treasures on earth, where moth and rust destroy and where thieves break in and steal; but lay up for yourselves treasures in heaven, where neither moth nor rust destroys and where thieves do not break in and steal. For where your treasure is, there your heart will be also. —Matthew 6:19–21

A dozen questions may be bouncing around the walls of your mind.

- How will I survive the sorrow I'll face?
- Am I better able to handle the stress now than I was before?
- How long am I going to struggle with depression and grief?
- Who can I talk to now that she's gone?

57

- With whom can I share my feelings, interests, and dreams?
- With whom can I share my special moments?
- What am I going to do with my time now that I'm alone?
- On whom can I depend now that he's gone?
- Who will take care of me?
- How can I stop thinking about the emptiness of my heart?
- Will my family and friends really satisfy my desires for intimacy?
- Isn't there anyone who wants or needs my love?
- Will I ever find the right person with whom I can share my life?

Most of these questions reveal an underlying anxiety about the future. But they also reveal the likelihood that one's dependence is focused on something other than God. On what are you building your trust? In whom are you placing your security?

If you are building your life around things that are temporal—things that can be taken away (as by thieves) or destroyed (as by moths or rust)—you will never truly be secure. There are no guarantees that the temporary things that God gives you to enjoy in this life will not be taken from you. Consequently, if you place your security in these kinds of treasures and they are taken away or destroyed, your whole world can easily come crashing in on you.

On the other hand, if you are building your life around treasures in heaven, which no one can take from you or destroy, then your world cannot be easily shaken.

If security comes from building one's life around things that endure for eternity rather than things that last for the moment, it follows that the more you build your life around temporal things, the more insecure you will be. The greater your security in the Lord, the greater will be your ability to "fall out of love." Conversely, the greater your insecurity, the greater will be your difficulty in getting over the breakup.

"All right, I see your point. But what exactly can I invest in down here that will still be intact when I get up there?"

There are several varieties of treasure that can be sent on ahead by the heavenly-minded believer. It is a great comfort to know that we have something better than the FDIC to protect our investments.

Heavenly Home Insurance

Will anyone or anything be able to take from you your relationship with Christ? Not if you truly are a Christian.

> For He Himself has said, "I will never leave you nor forsake you." (Heb. 13:5, quoting Josh. 1:5)

> I am persuaded that neither death nor life, nor angels nor principalities nor powers, nor things present nor things to come, nor height nor depth, nor any other created thing, shall be able to separate us from the love of God which is in Christ Jesus our Lord. (Rom. 8:38–39)

Will anyone or anything be able to destroy the Scriptures?

> Forever, O LORD,
> Your word is settled in heaven. (Ps. 119:89)

> Heaven and earth will pass away, but My words will by no means pass away. (Matt. 24:35)

> All flesh is as grass, and all the glory of man as the flower of the grass. The grass withers, and its flower falls away, but the word of the LORD endures forever. (1 Peter 1:24–25, quoting Isa. 40:6–8)

Will anyone or anything be able to destroy your service for God? The time and effort you spend ministering to others—

(people to whom you witness,[1] those you encourage and build up in the Lord, those you pray for, and those to whom you minister in countless other tangible and intangible ways)—will earn you rewards in heaven that cannot be taken away or destroyed, as long as your motives for ministry are truly to please and glorify God (cf. 1 Cor. 4:5; 2 John 8).

> He who receives a prophet in the name of a prophet shall receive a prophet's reward. And he who receives a righteous man in the name of a righteous man shall receive a righteous man's reward. And whoever gives one of these little ones only a cup of cold water in the name of a disciple, assuredly, I say to you, he shall by no means lose his reward. (Matt. 10:41–42)

> Now he who plants and he who waters are one, and each one will receive his own reward according to his own labor. (1 Cor. 3:8)

And what about your character? As you cooperate with the Spirit's sanctifying work of transforming you into the image of Christ, you are laying up for yourself treasures in heaven. "Discipline yourself for the purpose of godliness; for bodily discipline is only of little profit, but godliness is profitable for all things, since it holds promise for the present life and also for the life to come" (1 Tim. 4:7–8 NASB; cf. Matt. 25:21, 23; Rom. 2:7; 1 Cor. 4:5).

The main point of the book of Ecclesiastes is that there is no lasting security in this life. As Christians, we realize that our lasting pleasures and rewards come in the next life, not this one. The things that God gives us to enjoy down here (a loving spouse, a good meal, the satisfaction that comes from our labor, etc.) are temporary blessings to encourage us on our journey, but the real rewards come later in heaven.

But if you set your affections on the things of the earth rather than the things above (Col. 3:1–2), you will be profoundly disappointed. Even if moths or rust do not take away those temporal things, you will lose them when you die. They were meant to be only temporary comforts to sustain you on your way to heaven. As Richard Baxter pointed out over three hundred years ago:

> Remember for what purposes all worldly things were made and given. . . . They are the provisions of our bodies; our traveling equipment and aids; our hotels and comforting companions for the journey; they are God's love-tokens, some of the smaller coins from His storehouse that bear His image and inscription. They are drops from the rivers of eternal pleasures; to call to mind by way of our senses how good and amiable the Giver is—and what higher delights there are [for us in heaven], and to point us to the better things which these foreshadow. . . .
>
> They are the tools by which we must do much of our Master's work. They are means by which we may refresh our brethren, and express our love to one another, and our love to our Lord and Master in His service. They are our Master's stock, which we must trade with (and by which we may obtain the reward of endless happiness if we invest them profitably). These are the purposes for which God gives us outward mercies. Love them accordingly, and delight in them, and use them to these ends, and spare not—yes, seek them for such purposes and be thankful for them. But when God's provisions have been created for such excellent uses, will you debase them all by making them only the fuel for your lusts, and the provisions for your flesh? And will you love them and dote upon them in these carnal ways; while you utterly neglect their noblest uses?[2]

Have you been viewing the temporal provisions that God has momentarily supplied to you as items intended to be used for His glory and the benefit of others? Or have you seen them only as possessions given to you for your own benefit and pleasure?

How about your ex? Have you been looking at him as your own personal possession or as someone God has loaned to you for His purposes to accomplish His good will, not only in your life but also in His kingdom? Could it be that God's plan for this breakup extends far beyond your life and short-term personal happiness to the long-term eternal wellbeing of others? If you are truly a child of God, you can and should count on its being so.

9

Is Your Imagination Running Away with You?

Now I want you to know, brothers, that what has happened to me has really served to advance the gospel.
—*Philippians 1:12 NIV*

Are you struggling with vain regrets? Vain regrets are painful thoughts about the past (or what might have been in the future) that so dominate your thinking that they keep you from living biblically, responsibly, and productively in the present.[1] Such regrets are vain in the sense that they are worthless, futile, and fruitless. Nothing productive comes from them. Here are some examples of such thoughts.

- I just can't go on without her.
- If only I had done _____, maybe we'd still be together.
- If only I had not been so _____, maybe we'd still be together.

63

- If only he had been more _____, maybe we'd still be together.
- I'll never experience true love again.
- I'll always miss doing all those fun things we used to do together.
- I know I'll never find another person like her to love me.
- Why couldn't things have worked out?
- Nothing will ever be the same again.

If you are continually reviewing the hurtful consequences of your broken relationship, analyzing them, scrutinizing them, magnifying them, condemning yourself because of them, and projecting them into the future, you are letting your imagination run away with you. Stop torturing yourself with the past. Learn to replace such unwholesome thinking about yourself, your ex, and your God with thoughts that are true, honest, just, and pure.

God always builds the future on the past. Regardless of how bad that past may have been, He is able to give you "beauty for ashes" (Isa. 61:3) and "restore to you the years that the swarming locust has eaten" (Joel 2:25).

You can experience a life that is a testimony to Christ's transforming power. But if you focus your attention on the pain of the past rather than on how the Lord can build a bright future upon a dismal past, you may never see the beauty of such a life. Instead you may experience a future filled with self-pity, bitterness, doubt, depression, and despair. Some people have actually departed from the faith[2] as a result of not responding biblically to a difficult situation that God providentially brought into their lives. Other individuals have surrendered to God's sovereign will for their lives, faced the failures and heartaches of the past with the assurance that God was working all things together for their good, and in faith persevered until they saw God glorify Himself through a future that they could never have imagined.

"I really find it difficult to imagine how God can make something good come out of this breakup." Sometimes we have to take things by faith—believing what the Bible says is true even when we can't imagine how it could be so.

Put Yourself in Joseph's Sandals

Joseph was wrongly imprisoned after being falsely accused of forcing himself on Potiphar's wife. Have you ever stopped to consider what might have happened if Joseph had gotten what he wanted when he wanted it?

After interpreting the dreams of two of the king's officials, Joseph was hoping to be let out of prison immediately. "But when all goes well with you, remember me and show me kindness; mention me to Pharaoh and get me out of this dungeon," he said to the cupbearer who was about to be restored to his position (Gen. 40:14). *Any day now,* he probably told himself, *I'll be out of here. Surely that's why the Lord sent these men across my path and allowed me to interpret their dreams.* Imagine his disappointment as weeks turned into months and months into two full years without a word from anyone in Pharaoh's court concerning his release.

But think what would have happened if God had set Joseph free soon after the cupbearer was released from prison. It would have ruined the whole story! Joseph would almost certainly have run back to his family in Canaan, and that would have been that. Would there have been a happy ending? Perhaps, but Joseph's vindication would not have been so profound. His position as the number-two man in all of Egypt would have been given to another, his lifesaving ministry to his family and the vast number of people from other nations who were affected by the drought would have been wiped out, and most importantly, God's glory would not have been so prodigiously displayed for countless generations.

Imagine how the story might have ended if Joseph had allowed himself to be filled with self-pity and vain regrets. *I can't believe God allowed this to happen to me. That cupbearer! What a loser! I wish I'd never been given the gift of interpretation. It's only gotten me into trouble ever since I was a child. I should never have told anyone about that dream I had where my parents and brothers were bowing down to me. Boy, did I ever misinterpret that one! See if I ever offer to translate a dream for anyone else. If only I hadn't gone into Potiphar's house that day. I should have at least checked to see if anyone else was in the house before I went in. Why did I even bother to resist his wife? I probably wouldn't be here today if I wasn't such a righteous man. I just know I'll never get out of this place.*

Of course, we don't know what went through his mind, but remember, whatever it was, ultimately he was able to say to his brothers, "You meant evil against me, but God meant it for good *in order to bring about this present result*, to preserve many people alive" (Gen. 50:20 NASB).

Put Yourself in Paul's Prison

Joseph was not the only one in Scripture who was unjustly placed in prison. As Paul wrote the book of Philippians, he was sitting in a dungeon, fettered to a guard around the clock. The Romans had incarcerated him for more than two years. The Philippians could not understand why God was allowing this man, whom they loved deeply and who had been used so mightily to minister to them and many others, to waste away in a jail. *Why is God doing this to him? If anyone ought to be free, it's Paul! How will the church survive with its greatest missionary sidelined?* They couldn't figure out why God had allowed the gospel message to be stifled by this turn of events.

What if Paul had allowed his mind to be consumed with similar questions and vain regrets? *What a waste! Here I am,*

66

an apostle of Christ, chained to this guard in this dark, dank dungeon when I could be out and about doing the work of the kingdom! I don't know why God bothered to give me all these gifts if He's not going to let me use them. This is not the way I thought I'd be serving the Lord! Paul the apostle: missionary to the Praetorian Guard—what a joke! And all those people who trusted Christ as a result of my ministry—what's to become of them? If only I had listened to all those people who warned me about going to Jerusalem, I'd be free to proclaim the gospel the way it should be proclaimed! I don't know what possessed me to appeal to Caesar. What was I thinking? I should have taken my chances with the lower courts.

But Paul had a different angle on God's providence. Unlike the Philippians, he interpreted the circumstances into which God had placed him with hope. Taking himself and his personal concerns out of the equation, he was able to focus on how God was using the miserable conditions of his imprisonment to advance His kingdom. "I want you to know, brothers, that what has happened to me has really served to advance the gospel" (Phil. 1:12 NIV). Paul then proceeds to support his claim with two pieces of evidence. First, "the entire Praetorian Guard" (sixteen thousand men), as well as "everyone else" in the emperor's palace (the cooking and cleaning staff, groundskeepers, stable hands, and who knows how many others), had been exposed to the gospel of Christ (v. 13 NIV). Second, "most of the brethren in the Lord, having become confident" as a result of Paul's imprisonment, were "much more bold to speak the word without fear" (v. 14). Men who previously lacked courage were stepping forward to preach the gospel. Consequently, many more preachers went forth to proclaim the Word.

The apostle Paul can teach us another important lesson about handling vain regrets. Can you imagine how he might have been tempted to beat himself up about the way he persecuted Christ and His church? *What a blind, zealous fool I was! If only I had studied the Scriptures more carefully, I would have realized that Jesus really was the Messiah before I started throwing Christians into jail. If only I hadn't been there when Stephen was stoned to death. I just know I'm going to run into someone I persecuted or whose loved one I helped put to death.* But Paul didn't focus on the past. He focused on the present.

> Then last of all He was seen by me also, as by one born out of due time. For I am the least of the apostles, who am not worthy to be called an apostle, because I persecuted the church of God. But by the grace of God *I am what I am*, and His grace toward me was not in vain; but I labored more abundantly than they all, yet not I, but the grace of God which was with me. (1 Cor. 15:8–10)

He says, "I am what I am," not "I was what I was" or "I am what I was," because it didn't matter much to him what he used to be (c.f. 1 Cor. 6:9–11). Paul realized that the Lord was using his past to glorify Himself in a uniquely powerful way.

D. Martyn Lloyd-Jones comments on this passage in his book *Spiritual Depression*.

> "I am what I am"—whatever the past may have been. It is what I am that matters. What am I? I am forgiven, I am reconciled to God by the Blood of His Son upon the Cross. I am a child of God. I am adopted into God's family, and I am an heir with Christ, a joint-heir with Him. I am going to glory. That is what matters, not what I was, not what I have been. Do what the Apostle did therefore if the enemy is attacking you along this line. Turn to him and say: 'What you are saying is perfectly true. I was all you say. But what I am interested in is not what I was but what I am, and "I am what I am by the grace of God."[3]

Does your broken relationship hold you in its grip through vain regrets? You can put an end to the misery by focusing on the present rather than on the past, and by looking to the future with eyes of faith and hope in God's ability to cause all things to work together for your good. So from now on, when you think about your breakup and the impact it may have on your life, don't get historical—get hopeful!

10

It's Not the End
of the World

*We are hard pressed on every side, yet not crushed; we are
perplexed, but not in despair. —2 Corinthians 4:8*

Despair is one of the most debilitating emotions that people can experience. If you don't fight it, it can rob you of one of the essential ingredients for your stability as a Christian: hope. "I would have lost heart [NASB: *despaired*], unless I had believed that I would see the goodness of the LORD in the land of the living" (Ps. 27:13). For this reason, I typically spend the better part of almost every initial counseling session trying to give counselees hope. Sometimes that's all I do in the first session because it is such an important element for spiritual growth, especially during times of suffering.

Unlike the English word *hope*, which has a certain amount of uncertainty to it ("I hope I get through this trial, but after all, I'm only human"), the New Testament Greek word for *hope* denotes certainty ("I have confidence that by God's grace I'm going to come out on the other side of this trial a stronger person because that is what the Lord has promised in His Word").

The apostle Paul often found himself in perplexing situations. Paul didn't always understand what God was up to in every circumstance. He didn't always know how to interpret the specifics of his trials and was therefore somewhat limited at times in knowing exactly how to respond to them. But although he was *perplexed*, he did not *despair* because he knew enough about God's attributes (e.g., sovereignty, goodness, faithfulness) that he could trust God to work out everything for His glory and Paul's own ultimate good. He may have been, as the Greek words imply, "at a loss" to explain what was happening but not "totally at a loss" so as to lose hope. He may not have known with certainty what was going to happen next, but he certainly knew that God was in his circumstances working all things according to His predetermined plan (cf. Acts 2:23).

That's the secret of finding hope. One's ability to find hope in a seemingly hopeless situation is directly related to the ability to see God's hand in that situation. If you are despairing as a result of a broken relationship, you are not focusing on what God intends to do in your life, and for His kingdom, as a result of it.

"But I'm not a prophet or the son of a prophet. How in the world am I supposed to know what God is up to?"

You may not know what the future holds, but God has identified, in the Bible, some of the things He can do as a result of trials and tribulations—if you submit yourself to His agenda. Use your imagination to put the best possible interpretation on what God may be doing in your life. See this breakup with as much optimism as the Bible allows. Come up with the best biblical prognosis you can. Remember, love "believes all things" (1 Cor. 13:7). Love puts the best interpretation on the facts.

If we are to put a positive spin on the things that other sinners do, how much more should we translate the providence of God in the best imaginable light? Rather than allowing your mind to interpret God as dealing with you in ways that produce despair ("He intends to make me miserable" or "He's never going to allow me to be happy"), if you love Him you will (by believing the best) interpret God's providence according to His true character—in ways that produce hope.

"I see your point. If I love God, I'll believe He's going to bless me through this mess. But what *exactly* might God be up to in the termination of a romantic relationship?"

You can be certain that He is going to make you happier as a result of this breakup.

"How can you say that! That sounds presumptuous—and a little bit like 'name it-claim it' theology—if you ask me!"

I can say it because ultimately happiness is a direct result of obedience to Scripture. Jesus said, "Blessed [or *happy*] are those who hear the word of God and keep it!" (Luke 11:28). As you and I become conformed to the image of Christ, we become better equipped to handle the trials of life biblically and consequently experience greater joy, peace, and happiness in the midst of them. The more you become conformed to the image of Christ as a result of responding biblically to trials, the more those sinful patterns that the Bible says produce misery will be removed from your life. The degree of misery will be replaced with the same degree of happiness. As Peter put it, "He who has suffered in the flesh has ceased from sin, that he no longer should live the rest of his time in the flesh for the lusts of men, but for the will of God" (1 Peter 4:1–2). The more you live for God's will rather than for your own desires, the greater will be your measure of happiness.

Be Prepared

Trials also prepare us for greater ministry.

Blessed be the God and Father of our Lord Jesus Christ, the Father of mercies and God of all comfort, who comforts us in all our tribulation, that we may be able to comfort those who are in any trouble, with the comfort with which we ourselves are comforted by God. (2 Cor. 1:3–4)

One of God's sovereign designs for your breakup is to better prepare you to assist (*comfort*) others with the assistance that He (through the Holy Spirit) will be giving you. This may not excite you right now ("I really wasn't looking for that kind of ministry"), but down the road, you will appreciate it as you experience the joy and satisfaction of helping others, not just with breakup issues but with a variety of other problems. (The passage says that we will be better equipped to comfort those who are in *any* trouble.)

And consider another possibility. The Lord might be preparing you for marriage. He may have allowed this breakup so that He could put His finger on some flaws in your character that could hinder your future relationships, in particular marriage. God builds the future on the past.

There's also the matter of strengthening your relationship with God—learning how to better depend on Him and have fellowship with Him. Our God is a *living* God who desires to be intimately involved in our lives. He desires us to worship Him in *spirit* as well as in truth. He wants us to have fellowship with Him through prayer and the Word. (We talk to God in prayer and He talks to us in the Bible.) Much of the extra time you now have on your hands as a result of the breakup can be spent in more fellowship with the Lord. Do you long to spend hours each week enjoying the fellowship of your former companion? Perhaps the Lord wants you to take a few of those hours and spend them with Him. The more time you spend with God in the Word and prayer, the greater will be your peace, your strength, and your hope for the future. You will come to know Him better and perhaps, like Paul, know more fully "the power of His resurrection, and the fellowship of His sufferings" (Phil. 3:10).

What else could God be up to in your life as a result of your breakup? The possibilities are endless. On the following page is a worksheet on which you can record any additional ways in which God may be working in your life. See how many you can come up with.

Before you start, let me give you a word of caution. God is not obligated to tell you what He is up to. He apparently never told Job the exact purpose for his suffering. Don't make the same mistake Job did by demanding from God an explanation. Elihu wisely asked Job, "Why do you complain against Him that He does not give an account of all His doings?" (Job 33:13 NASB).

Are you perplexed or confused by the breakup? It's not a sin to be perplexed. Are you despairing? If so, that is a problem. Don't give in to your feelings. Don't give up. And whatever you do, don't stop reading this book. There is more hope and help for overcoming despair in the next chapter.

THINGS THAT GOD MAY BE DOING IN MY LIFE
AS A RESULT OF MY BROKEN RELATIONSHIP

1. God is conforming me to the image of Christ, which will ultimately result in His glory and my happiness.
2. God is preparing me for future ministry.
3. God is preparing me for future relationships—perhaps even the ultimate human relationship: marriage.
4. God is strengthening my dependence on and my walk with Him.
5. _____
   _____
6. _____
   _____
7. _____
   _____
8. _____
   _____
9. _____
   _____
10. _____
    _____
11. _____
    _____
12. _____
    _____

11

What Good Comes to the Brokenhearted?

Therefore, since we have this ministry, as we have received
mercy, we do not lose heart. —2 Corinthians 4:1

If anyone had a right to be discouraged about life, it was the apostle Paul. Here are a few of the discouraging things that Paul had to endure.

> From the Jews five times I received forty stripes minus one. Three times I was beaten with rods; once I was stoned; three times I was shipwrecked; a night and a day I have been in the deep; in journeys often, in perils of waters, in perils of robbers, in perils of my own countrymen, in perils of the Gentiles, in perils in the city, in perils in the wilderness, in perils in the sea, in perils among false brethren; in weariness and toil, in sleeplessness often, in hunger and thirst, in fastings often, in cold and nakedness—besides the other things, what comes upon me daily: my deep concern for all the churches. (2 Cor. 11:24–28)

How did Paul keep from despairing over his circumstances? The answer is found in the first verse of 2 Corinthians 4. He focused on the ministry that God had given him to fulfill. "Therefore, since we have this *ministry*, as we have received mercy, *we do not lose heart.*"

The original Greek verb translated "to lose heart" carries with it a nuance of fear or cowardliness that does not usually make it into English translations. It is a kind of despondency that comes through (or as a result of) fear.[1] Fear tempts us to say, "It's too hard," "I quit," or "I can't go on." Paul didn't make a habit of giving in to this temptation. Rather, he focused on the responsibilities that God had given him and thereby overcame any despondency-producing fear.[2]

I am indebted to my good friend Jay Adams for opening my eyes to this life-transforming principle.

> Paul did not become depressed, because he had learned to handle affliction and trouble God's way. Those who do, do not need to become depressed. He could write, "We are afflicted in all sorts of ways, but not crushed; perplexed, but not given to despair" (v. 8). Even the most extreme pressures did not lead to depression.
>
> What was it that made the difference? The clue that leads to the answer is found in the first part of the first verse: **Therefore, since we have this service to perform as the result of mercy**, Paul says, "We don't give up." His gratitude to God impelled him to continue in the service (ministry) to which He had called him, no matter what happened. He knew that he deserved nothing from God but wrath. How grateful, therefore, he was for the mercy that had been shown him in pure grace, not only saving, but also putting him into the service of Christ in such a prominent way. Because of that gratitude he would carry on his ministry to the end. He would continue, though left in a pile of stones for dead at Lystra, though shipwrecked, though lashed, though imprisoned. . . . He would continue to preach

the gospel world-round until his Lord said "enough." He was wholly at the beck and call of the One who had called him in the first place. Cowardice faded under the bright light of gratitude.[3]

Do you give in to your feelings of fear and despondency or do you fight them by fulfilling your responsibilities no matter how you feel? When you give in to your feelings, you will give up on your responsibilities. When you give up on your responsibilities, you will feel guilty. The more you give in and give up, the guiltier you will feel. The guiltier you feel, the more depressed you will become. But if you fulfill your responsibilities (however feebly), you will foil depression before it has a chance to take a foothold in your life.

Long ago, I "fell in love" with a young lady who unilaterally terminated our dating relationship and broke my heart. What did I do to help ease the pain? Even though my heart was experiencing agonizing pain, I went to work every day and made myself focus on the problems of my counselees.

It didn't immediately remove all my sorrow. In fact, sometimes I could hardly pay attention because of the distracting thoughts of sorrow that kept fighting for my attention. On some days, it seemed that I was operating at only 40 percent efficiency. But day by day, my ministry to others served as a catalyst to speed up the healing of my broken heart. The more I concentrated on helping others solve their problems, the less time I spent focusing on my own grief. Moreover, the joy that came as a result of seeing God use me—especially in such a weakened condition—was a wonderful balm that eased the pain of my aching heart.

> Blessed be the God and Father of our Lord Jesus Christ, the Father of compassion and God of all help, who helps us in all our afflictions to make us capable of helping persons in every sort of affliction by the help with which God helped us. (2 Cor. 1:3–4 CCNT)

God is in the process of preparing you for future ministry through this breakup. Don't wait until then to get started. If you're not already doing so, begin right now to serve others.

WAYS I CAN SERVE OTHERS THROUGH THIS TRIAL

In the spaces below, list those individuals whom you may be able to serve in specific ways. Next to each name, identify how you can most effectively minister to that person.

Person to Serve   Types of Service

_____   _____

                                   _____

                                   _____

_____   _____

                                   _____

_____   _____

                                   _____

_____   _____

                                   _____

_____   _____

                                   _____

12

I *Can* Get Used to Losing You

*Because I have said these things to you,
sorrow has filled your heart. —John 16:6*

The breakup of a relationship may involve not only the loss of close companionship but also a loss of emotional support, comfort, security, reputation, and more. If you're not careful, losses such as these can overshadow your entire outlook and cause you to be overcome with sorrow.

Before His death, Jesus gave His disciples some disturbing information. He told them not only that the days ahead would involve considerable difficulty, but that He would no longer be with them. For quite some time, these men had had a special relationship with the Lord and a very real hope that He would be establishing His kingdom on earth in the immediate future.

How did they respond when they realized that their hopes were about to be dashed? Their hearts became *filled with sorrow*.

"But because I have said these things to you, sorrow has filled your heart." The word *filled* implies a kind of filling that is complete. It is to fill to a full measure—or, as we might say, to "fill to the brim." When something is filled that completely, there is room for nothing else. When a heart is filled with sorrow, the sorrow so completely occupies one's life that it displaces everything else.

Now, there's nothing wrong with a little bit of sorrow. In fact, Jesus was "a Man of sorrows and acquainted with grief" (Isa. 53:3). Yet He also had an abundance of peace, joy, and love. He was able to say such things as "My peace I give to you" (John 14:27), "These things I have spoken to you, that My joy may remain in you, and that your joy may be full" (John 15:11), and "As the Father loved Me, I also have loved you; abide in My love" (John 15:9). So a certain amount of sorrow may simultaneously abide with love, joy, and peace in one's heart.

Jesus never let His sorrow prevent Him from fulfilling any of His responsibilities. That is, He never allowed His sorrow to become so great that it totally shut Him down. "Now My soul is troubled, and what shall I say? 'Father, save Me from this hour'? But for this purpose I came to this hour" (John 12:27).

In the garden of Gethsemane, Jesus told His disciples, "My soul is exceedingly sorrowful, even to death. Stay here and watch with Me" (Matt. 26:38). He then proceeded to pray so agonizingly that "His sweat became like great drops of blood" (Luke 22:44). His disciples, on the other hand, had allowed their sorrow to keep them from fully discharging the responsibilities He had just given them.

> Coming out, He went to the Mount of Olives, as He was accustomed, and His disciples also followed Him. When He came to the place, He said to them, *"Pray that you may not enter into temptation."* And He was withdrawn from them about a stone's throw, and He knelt down and prayed, saying, "Father, if it is Your will, take this cup away from Me; nevertheless not My will, but Yours, be done." Then an angel appeared to Him from heaven, strengthening Him. And being in agony, He prayed more earnestly. Then His sweat became like great drops of blood falling down to the ground. When He rose up from prayer, and had come to His disciples, He found them *sleeping from sorrow.* Then He said to them, "Why do you sleep? Rise and pray, lest you enter into temptation." (Luke 22:39–46)

The disciples were exhausted as a result of their sorrow. Yet Jesus admonished them for sleeping and commanded them to get back to work. When we are faced with any loss, it is normal for us to grieve. As Solomon said, "Sorrow is better than laughter, for by a sad countenance the heart is made better" (Eccl. 7:3).

The danger comes when we allow our grief to become so great that it overpowers other things in our lives that God says we ought not to let slip. When experiencing heartaches, we can easily allow sorrow to fill our lives to such an extent that we stop thinking about those things that generate love, joy, peace, or any other element of the Spirit's fruit. Our sorrow must not quench the Spirit's work in our lives. We ought not grieve so much that we stop fulfilling our biblical responsibilities or avoid our ministry opportunities. Rather than allow our sorrow to control us, we should continue to be controlled by the Spirit. To be "filled with the Spirit" (Eph. 5:18) is to be controlled by the Spirit. To be filled with sorrow is to be controlled by sorrow.

"But what if I'm already there? What if I've allowed my heart to be filled, or almost filled, with sorrow to the point that I'm shutting down mentally and emotionally?"

Then by the Spirit's enabling power, you will have to work hard at getting your sorrow back down to a manageable level. First, think the kinds of thoughts that will generate the right kinds of feelings. "Whatever things are true, whatever things are noble, whatever things are just, whatever things are pure, whatever things are lovely, whatever things are of good report, if there is any virtue and if there is anything praiseworthy—meditate on these things" (Phil. 4:8). Rather than thinking only of what you've lost, think about how God may be using your loss to benefit you. Rather than thinking about how miserable you are, ponder how you can make someone else happy. Rather than worrying about what will happen to you tomorrow, figure out how you can be a blessing to someone today. Instead of grumbling and complaining, praise God for all the things He has done for you.

The second thing you can do to help get your sorrow under control is to fulfill your biblical responsibilities. If you are not already doing so, get involved in ministering to others. Yes, you can do these things even though your heart is sorrowful. It may not be easy, and it won't be fun at first. But in time, your mind will be occupied with more noble thoughts than your own grief. The satisfaction that comes from being responsible and the joy that comes from serving others will begin to refill your heart as it displaces your superfluous grief.

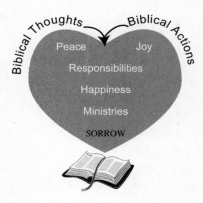

Take a few minutes right now to make a list of any responsibilities you've been neglecting as a result of being consumed with the loss of your relationship. Then write out Philippians 4:8. List those things you can meditate on when you are tempted to think about all you've lost. (Perhaps the first entry should be "things to put on my Philippians 4:8 list.") Put this list in your wallet or purse and carry it with you wherever you go.

13

I Just Called to Say, "I *Don't* Love You!"

Let all bitterness, wrath, anger, clamor, and evil speaking be put away from you, with all malice. —Ephesians 4:31

How did you respond to the rejection you experienced as a result of the breakup? The rejection you felt may have come not only from your ex, but from your mutual friends or his family.

Let's "zoom out" for a moment and look at your responses to rejection with a wide-angle lens. How do you usually respond when you are rejected or hurt?

Each of us desires certain intangible expressions of love such as respect, appreciation, approval, praise, and commendation. The Bible assumes that each of us naturally finds a certain measure of delight in these things. The problem occurs, however, when we delight in them too much.

Ask yourself, "Did this person really sin against me?" If someone has sinned against you, there are two options available to you. You may choose to overlook it or cover it in love (Prov. 17:9; 1 Peter 4:8). If you are unable to overlook it, follow Luke 17:3. "If your brother sins against you, rebuke him; and if he repents, forgive him." That is, pursue your offender with the intent of granting him forgiveness when he acknowledges his sin. But if you were hurt as a result of that which was not a sin, *you* must repent of your unbiblical thinking that caused you to be too easily offended.

In Ephesians 4:31, the apostle Paul identified half a dozen sinful ways in which people tend to respond in the midst of relationship difficulties.

Sinful Responses to Rejection

The first response is **bitterness**. This word literally describes the bitter taste of certain food and drink. The verb translated "to be bitter" means "to cut" or "to prick." You may think of the word *bitterness* as an inward resentment or unforgiving spirit, and so it is. But this inward attitude will cut and prick others as well. "See to it that no one comes short of the grace of God; that no root of bitterness springing up causes trouble, and by it *many* be defiled" (Heb. 12:15 NASB). Bitterness is the result of not forgiving others. If you are bitter at your ex, it is an indication that you haven't truly forgiven him/her.

The second response is **wrath**. This word has a broad range of meaning. Its most basic meaning has to do with "a vital force." It is heated, passionate, furious anger that quickly boils up and almost as quickly subsides. This is a sudden outburst of anger—like a cherry bomb that explodes once and then is spent. When a person responds with this kind of anger, doors may be slammed, feet may stomp, people may be punched or kicked, items may be thrown and broken, voices may be raised, names may be hurled, unrighteous expletives may be used, and false accusations may abound.

A good example of this overactive, volatile, explosive, eruptive anger is found in the second chapter of Matthew. This is the account of the magi who were following a special star that was to lead them to the Christ child.

> Then Herod secretly called the magi and determined from them the exact time the star appeared. And he sent them to Bethlehem and said, "Go and search carefully for the Child; and when you have found Him, report to me, so that I too may come and worship Him." After hearing the king, they went their way. . . . And having been warned by God in a dream not to return to Herod, the magi left for their own country by another way. . . . Then when Herod saw that he had been *tricked* by the magi, he became *very enraged*, and sent and *slew all the male children* who were in Bethlehem and all its vincinity, from two years old and under, according to the time which he had determined from the magi. (Matt. 2:7–9, 12, 16 NASB)

Anger is the third descriptive word used in our text. It has two basic meanings.

The more general and broad meaning is an upsurge of emotion that sometimes manifests itself in impulsive actions—especially vindictive or punitive actions. It's an inner disposition that produces not only impulsivity, but also intense passion—outward expressions of displeasure and anger. It's much easier to act impulsively right after being hurt or rejected by others than it is in more affable circumstances. This intense passion that can result from wrong thinking in response to the offense can be quite powerful and destructive.

The more specific meaning of this word is a less volatile and less episodic but more enduring kind of anger. This is a state of mind—a condition of the soul. It is the kind of anger that, if left unchecked, produces characterological anger[1] and turns its possessor into an angry man. This kind of anger is the slow-boil variety.

When this person is hurt or rejected, he doesn't usually react violently. In fact, he may even withdraw. When you ask him if he is angry, he may well respond with, "No, I'm just a little *hurt*." This kind of internalized anger can be so subtle that you may have a difficult time detecting it in your own heart.

The fourth common response to being rejected is **clamor**. This is a public outcry, a tumult. (The verb means "to croak.") The person who is clamoring is griping, complaining, and belly-aching in a rabble-rousing, agitating sort of way. There is a vivid illustration of the effects of this kind of public instigation in the book of Acts.

> About that time there occurred *no small disturbance*[2] concerning the Way. For a man named Demetrius, a silversmith, who made silver shrines of Artemis, was bringing no little business to the craftsmen; these he *gathered together*[3] with the workmen of similar trades, and said, "Men, you know that our prosperity depends upon this business. You see and hear that not only in Ephesus, but in almost all of Asia, this Paul has persuaded and turned away a considerable number of people, saying that gods made with hands are no gods at all. Not only is there danger that this trade of ours fall into disrepute, but also that the temple of the great goddess Artemis be regarded as worthless and that she whom all of Asia and the world worship will even be dethroned from her magnificence."
>
> When they heard this and were *filled* with *rage*, they began *crying out*, saying, "Great is Artemis of the Ephesians!" The city was *filled* with the *confusion* . . . (Acts 19:23–29 NASB)

The fifth item in our text is **slander** or **evil speaking**. The Greek (*blasphemia*) is a compound word that combines the concept of hurt, injury, or harm with speech. This term involves speech that is abusive, defaming, or harmful to another's good name. It is used to describe the strongest form of mockery or slander. Whereas clamor speaks of a more public form of criticism, slander or evil-speaking may occur between as few as two people.

What have you told others about your ex? Have you been guilty of clamor or gossip? I realize that she may have done you much wrong, but you may not respond in kind. The apostle Peter said:

> Finally, all of you be of one mind, having compassion for one another; love as brothers, be tenderhearted, be courteous; not returning evil for evil or reviling for reviling, but on the contrary blessing, knowing that you were called to this, that you may inherit a blessing. For
>
> "He who would love life
> And see good days,
> Let him refrain his tongue from evil,
> And his lips from speaking deceit.
> Let him turn away from evil and do good;
> Let him seek peace and pursue it."
> (1 Peter 3:8–11, quoting Ps. 34:12–14)

The last item on our list is **malice**. The word has a variety of meanings, including maliciousness, hatred, resentment, ill feeling, ill will, and the desire to injure. Malice holds grudges. Herodias had this kind of malice for John the Baptist. The hatred she held against him for condemning her incestuous marriage to Herod ultimately manifested itself in murder. "Herodias had a grudge against him and wanted to put him to death and could not do so" (Mark 6:19 NASB). The Greek word for "had a grudge against" can also be translated "held it against" or "had it in for." If you're holding something against your ex or somehow "have it in for" him, you may be flirting with malice.

So which kind of anger best describes your response to being hurt or rejected? Do you resemble a bitter root, a cherry bomb, a pot of boiling water, a public croaker, or a grudge-holder?

"OK, I confess, I'm guilty of at least one or two of these. So what do I do now?"

Keep reading! The biblical solution to these problems (found in the next verse, Ephesians 4:32) is explained in the following two chapters.

14

Love Be Tender

And be kind to one another, tenderhearted, forgiving
one another, even as God in Christ forgave you.
—Ephesians 4:32

The verse above prescribes three antidotes to venomous anger. It provides three biblical imperatives for us to follow when we've been hurt or rejected by others.

The first response is to be **kind**. The word means to be good, pleasant, kind, merciful, and generous. Kindness encompasses the idea of loving one's enemies and doing good and lending without expecting repayment. It is being merciful even to those who have hurt us.

> But I say to you who hear: *Love* your enemies, *do good* to those who hate you, *bless* those who curse you, and *pray for* those who spitefully use you. To him who strikes you on the one cheek, *offer* the other also. And from him who takes away your cloak, *do not withhold* your tunic either. *Give* to everyone who asks of you. And from him who takes away your goods *do not ask them back*. And just as you want men to do to you, you also *do*

to them likewise. But if you love those who love you, what credit is that to you? For even sinners love those who love them. And if you do good to those who do good to you, what credit is that to you? For even sinners do the same. And if you lend to those from whom you hope to receive back, what credit is that to you? For even sinners lend to sinners to receive as much back. But *love your enemies, do good,* and lend, hoping for nothing in return; and your reward will be great, and you will be sons of the Most High. For He is *kind* to the unthankful and evil. Therefore *be merciful,* just as your Father also is *merciful.* (Luke 6:27–36)

In this passage, Christ gives a general order: "Love your enemies." In verses 27 and 28, He gives specific applications of that general order:

Application #1 Do good to those who hate you.
Application #2 Bless those who curse you.
Application #3 Pray for those who mistreat you.

He continues giving specific applications of this general command in verses 29 through 31.

Application #4 Whoever hits you on the cheek, offer him the other also.
Application #5 Whoever takes away your coat, do not withhold your shirt from him either.
Application #6 Give to everyone who asks of you, and whoever takes away what is yours, do not demand it back.
Application #7 Just as you want people to treat you, treat them in the same way. (This is a rule of thumb for loving your enemies.)

94

So in order to show kindness to the one who has hurt you, you must love him, do good to him, pray for him, praise him (where you can), turn the other cheek to him, go the second mile with him, give him what he needs. In other words, treat him exactly the way that you would want him to treat you. And if you do, regardless of what happens here on earth, your reward will be great in heaven.

"But how can I show acts of kindness to my ex, since we're not together anymore?"

Let me again refer you to Appendix E for some possible specific answers to your question.

Try a Little Tenderheartedness

The next word in our text is **tenderhearted**. A compound term that combines the word *good* with the word *guts* or *inward parts*, it means "full of compassion" or "having pity." It suggests a warm, tender feeling toward others.

> Finally, all of you be of one mind, having compassion for one another; love as brothers, be *tenderhearted*, be courteous; *not returning evil for evil or reviling for reviling, but on the contrary blessing*, knowing that you were called to this, that you may inherit a blessing. (1 Peter 3:8–9)

The context in which Peter uses the word *tenderhearted* is one of being offended. The person who is tenderhearted can look at his offenders much as Christ looked at His, focusing more on their needs than on His own. Do you do that with your ex? The tenderhearted person has compassion for the one who offended him because he realizes that the very sin that hurt him is probably hurting his offender even more. Have you ever thought about your ex with such compassion? A tenderhearted person is able to focus his thoughts and energy on ministering to his offender rather than getting even with him.

Of course, depending on your circumstances, this may need to be done from a distance. But if you cannot do anything else, you can always minister to her through prayer. You can pray that God will help her to grow as a Christian (or save him if he is lost). If she has sinned against you or others and has not yet acknowledged it, pray that the Holy Spirit will convict her of these things. You can pray that God will help her to see any unbiblical thoughts and motives in her heart. You can pray that God will send others to minister the Word to her and that he will be sheltered from any wrong influences. For additional ideas, you may want to study some of the prayers that the apostle Paul prayed for those he ministered to in various churches, such as the one he prayed on behalf of the Philippians:

> And this I pray, that your love may abound still more and more in knowledge and all discernment, that you may approve the things that are excellent, that you may be sincere and without offense till the day of Christ, being filled with the fruits of righteousness which are by Jesus Christ, to the glory and praise of God. (Phil. 1:9–11)

Your prayers for God's blessing on your ex not only will have impact on his/her life, but will profoundly affect your own heart as well, disposing you to be more naturally tenderhearted. Although care should be taken not to spend inordinate amounts of time praying for your ex lest the romantic feelings that you are trying to abate be rekindled, you will actually have more warm and tender feelings for him if you make such prayer a regular part of your life.

15

Won't Be Cruel

*And be kind to one another, tenderhearted, forgiving
one another, even as God in Christ forgave you.*
—Ephesians 4:32

We now come to what may be for you the most important chapter in this book—Bible basics about forgiveness.

"That's great, but I don't really see the connection between forgiveness and 'falling out of love.' Despite what I've learned so far, it still seems to me that a person would stand a better chance of getting rid of romantic feelings if he *hated* his ex than if he *forgave* her."

So you think it is better to displace feelings of love with feelings of hate?

"Well, it's probably not better. But for me, anger might be easier to handle than all this passion."

It will not be easier in the long run. The antithesis to forgiveness is not anger; it is bitterness. The more you hate your ex, the more bitter and resentful you will become. And then you'll find yourself getting angry more often than if you'd forgiven.

Bitterness is the result of responding improperly to a hurt. Take a look at Hebrews 12:15:

> See to it that no one comes short of the grace of God; that no root of bitterness springing up causes trouble, and by it many be defiled.

The Scripture likens bitterness to a root. Roots have to be planted. When someone hurts you,[1] it is as if a seed has been dropped onto the soil of your heart. You can choose to respond in two ways. You can either pluck out the seed by forgiving your offender, or you can begin to cultivate the seed by reviewing the hurt over and over in your mind. Bitterness is the result of dwelling too long on a hurt. It is the result of not truly forgiving an offender (cf., Matt. 18:34–35).[2]

Jane and Jimmy had dated for nine months. About the time Jane was expecting an engagement ring, she got a phone call from Jimmy, who was on one of his frequent business trips. He explained that his feelings for her had been changing over the past several months, and he suggested that they slow down the relationship and perhaps even start seeing other people.

Jane's seed of hurt could be easily transformed into a root of bitterness.

JANE'S INTERNAL MONOLOGUE	CULTIVATION OF JANE'S BITTERNESS
"I can't believe he's dumping me! He didn't even have the courage to tell me to my face but called on the telephone."	Jane presses the seed an inch or two into the soil of her heart.
"He's such a coward!"	Jane covers the seed with more soil.

"He calls himself a Christian? What a joke! I should have known better than to trust him with my heart."	Jane aerates the soil.
"He's so selfish. Like all men, he can't handle commitment."	Jane waters the seed.
"He has defrauded me. I never should have gotten involved with him."	Jane fertilizes her hurt, and it starts to sprout.
"How would he like it if I did that to him? I hope his next girlfriend tears his heart out."	Jane weeds her little sprout, and its roots grow deeper.
Jane starts singing to herself the words to a popular song about the sweetness of getting revenge.	Jane builds a greenhouse around her stinkweed and starts charging people admission to see it.

Regardless of what your ex has done to hurt you, as a Christian who is committed to pleasing God, you really have no choice but to forgive him of any sins that he has committed against you.

Bible Basics about Forgiveness

The principles that follow have been extrapolated mainly from Luke 17:3–10. Other passages have been cited where applicable.

> "Take heed to yourselves. If your brother sins against you, rebuke him; and if he repents, forgive him. And if he sins against you seven times in a day, and seven times in a day returns to you, saying, 'I repent,' you shall forgive him."
> And the apostles said to the Lord, "Increase our faith."

So the Lord said, "If you have faith as a mustard seed, you can say to this mulberry tree, 'Be pulled up by the roots and be planted in the sea,' and it would obey you. And which of you, having a servant plowing or tending sheep, will say to him when he has come in from the field, 'Come at once and sit down to eat'? But will he not rather say to him, 'Prepare something for my supper, and gird yourself and serve me till I have eaten and drunk, and afterward you will eat and drink'? Does he thank that servant because he did the things that were commanded him? I think not. So likewise you, when you have done all those things which you are commanded, say, 'We are unprofitable servants. We have done what was our duty to do.'"

Forgiveness is to be granted only if a sin has been committed against you.

Jesus said, "If your brother sins . . ." He didn't say, "If he doesn't give you what you want," "If he lets you down," "If he hurts your feelings," or "If he profoundly disappoints you." Your brother may do any and all of these things in the process of sinning, but he is not in need of your forgiveness unless he *sins* against you.[3]

Sometimes the offended party must initiate forgiveness.

If you cannot overlook the transgression (Prov. 19:11) or cover it in love (1 Peter 4:8), you are obligated as a Christian to go to a brother who has sinned against you and "rebuke him." Sometimes we must go to our sinning brother and tell him about his sin with the intention of being able to grant him forgiveness.

"But he sinned against me! Why does his sin obligate me to go to him? Didn't Jesus say somewhere that he is supposed to come to me before he brings his gift to the altar?"

He did. In Matthew 5:23–24, Jesus tells us to seek forgiveness from those whom we have offended. In that passage the *offending* party is told to go.

But we are looking at Luke chapter 17, which says that the *offended* party should go. Since you, as the offended party, are the one who has knowledge of the wrong, you are to go. The one who knows about the offense is the one who goes. Perhaps your ex doesn't know about her sin, or maybe she doesn't want to seek reconciliation. Or, as happens rather frequently, it could be that there is a misperception on someone's part that requires a discussion to clear up the issue. It might even be discovered that no real sin was actually committed.

Forgiveness is fundamentally a promise.

In his insightful book *From Forgiven to Forgiving*, Dr. Jay Adams explains:

> When God forgives, He goes on record. He says so. He declares, "I will not remember your sins" (Isa. 43:25; see also Jer. 31:34). Isn't that wonderful? When He forgives, God lets us know that He will no longer hold our sins against us. If forgiveness were merely an emotional experience, we would not know that we were forgiven. But praise God, we do, because forgiveness is a process at the end of which God declares that the matter of sin has been dealt with once for all.
>
> Now what is that declaration? What does God do when He goes on record saying that our sins are forgiven? God makes a promise. Forgiveness is not a feeling; forgiveness is a *promise!*[4]

When you forgive, you are promising to no longer hold your offender's trespasses against him. You are also promising to impute your forgiveness to him (much as Christ imputed His righteousness to you when you became a Christian). The dictionary defines *impute* as follows: "1) to charge with the fault or responsibility for; 2) to attribute or credit."[5] When you promise to not impute your offender's trespasses against him, you are promising to no longer charge him for what he has done. This means that you are not going to allow yourself to dwell on the offense. You will refuse to cultivate those seeds of hurt, but rather will immediately pluck them out of the soil of your heart.

When you promise to impute your forgiveness, you credit your offender's account with your forgiveness, much as Christ credited your heavenly account with His righteousness. You make every effort to think well of him, to pray for him, and, if possible, to speak well of him. These two promises can be made in the form of a personal commitment in your heart even if your offender does not acknowledge his sins to you. This is what is sometimes referred to as "forgiving someone in your heart" (cf. Mark 11:25).

If he does acknowledge his sins and asks for your forgiveness, you will make those promises to him as you verbally grant him forgiveness. In such a case, you will be making him two additional promises. Implicit in the "not remembering his sins" concept is a promise to not ever bring up the offense to him again. If you have forgiven him, there is no need to discuss it again. Similar sins that he may commit in the future may require new confrontations. In addition, when you verbally grant someone forgiveness, you are promising to not tell anyone else about the offense.[6]

Forgiveness is not the same as trust.

If someone sins against you, it is incumbent upon you as a Christian to forgive that person as you have been forgiven by God in Christ (cf. Matt. 18:21–35). However, it is incumbent upon that person to earn back the trust he lost as a result of his sin. Forgiveness should be immediate. Trust usually takes time. It would be foolish to trust someone who has struggled with a pattern of certain sins without giving her an opportunity to earn back the trust she has lost and thus prove herself faithful. To withhold trust after it has been earned is unloving, since love "believes all things" (1 Cor. 13:7; cf. Prov. 27:22; Jer. 13:23; Matt. 25:14–31; Luke 16:10–12).

Forgiveness involves an act of the will—not the emotions.

If your ex repents, you must forgive him—on the spot. Jesus phrased this in such a way as to make it clear that (in the absence of evidence to the contrary) you have to take your offender at his word and grant him forgiveness. Even if it is the seventh time in one day that he has asked you to do so, you are to forgive him (Luke 17:4). Jesus does not give you very much time to get your feelings in line *before* you forgive. You are to do it as an act of your will in obedience to God. Your feelings will follow. If you wait until your feelings subside before you forgive, you may never obey the Lord's command.

In Luke 17:5–10, the disciples had a hard time with Christ's teaching on this subject. Their response to Him was an incredulous "Increase our faith." They thought they needed more faith in order to obey this teaching. Through a parable, Christ instructed them that it was not more faith they needed, but rather more faithfulness. The slave in the story was not being asked to do something he was incapable of doing, despite how exhausted he might have *felt* after returning to his master's house from a long day's work. Preparing the evening meal was something that he was expected to do. It was not optional. It was not something for which he would be receiving time and a half as a consolation. Neither would he receive special commendation. It was his job! Forgiveness is a part of your job description, too. And like any job, forgiveness has some responsibilities that are easier and more enjoyable than others. Some you feel like doing; others you do whether or not you feel like doing them.

"But what if *after* I forgive her, I begin to have feelings of resentment toward her? I'll feel like such a hypocrite!"

You will not feel that way if you think biblically about the matter. After granting forgiveness, remind yourself that you made a promise to your ex. Don't let that seed of hurt develop into a root of bitterness by dwelling on it. Pray for her and put your mind into a Philippians 4:8 thought pattern: "Whatever things are true, whatever things are noble, whatever things are just, whatever things are pure, whatever things are lovely, whatever things are of good report, if there is any virtue and if there is anything praiseworthy—meditate on these things."

Rather than reviewing mental images from the past (seeing the face of your ex on a dartboard or on a golf ball), picture her face with the words "I've forgiven you" boldly imprinted across the image. Put your imagination to work on Philippians 4:8 (or other relevant passages of Scripture). You may be surprised at how much better you will feel. You may also be surprised at how much more quickly you will forget once you truly forgive. Forgetting is the result of forgiving, not the means of it. It is the final step of the process, not the first one.

16

Yesterday Wants More

*But put on the Lord Jesus Christ, and make no provision
for the flesh, to fulfill its lusts. —Romans 13:14*

A ndy was devastated by the breakup. He still loved Brooke.
He wanted her to change her mind and restore what they
once had together, although he knew that wasn't likely to happen. How was he going to get over her? Everywhere he looked
there were traces of love that tormented him as they triggered his
memory and stirred up old feelings. His apartment was filled with
mementos (photographs, gifts, cards and letters, ticket stubs, and
other souvenirs). Even things that had once been neutral (certain
foods, fragrances, and places around town) seemed associated
with her somehow.

Andy passed Brooke's favorite fast-food restaurant on his
way to and from work every day. He could hardly look at it
without thinking of her. And he wasn't about to go inside for
a meal because he was afraid of getting depressed. He avoided
it for months after the breakup. Then one day on his lunch

break, he said to himself, "This is crazy. It's only a restaurant. I can't spend the rest of my life avoiding things that remind me of Brooke. I'll just have to make some new memories of this place."

So Andy went in, ordered his lunch, and found that it wasn't as difficult as he had imagined it would be. He discovered that it was relatively easy to make new and pleasant memories of places that formerly had unpleasant ones.

What are some of the reminders in your life that make it difficult for you to stop thinking about your ex? What are you doing about them? Some items can be returned or removed. For those reminders that are more permanent (like restaurants, stores, and houses), you will have to make new associations.

The Bible instructs us to "make no provision for the flesh, to fulfill its lusts" (Rom. 13:14). To "make provision" for something is to *exercise forethought about* or to *plan ahead to do* something. Paul commands us to stop planning ahead so as to satisfy the desires of our flesh.[1]

"But I'm not planning to do anything wrong. I'm not really planning to do anything. These reminders are just all over the place."

I realize that you probably haven't left things around in your life just to remind yourself of your ex. But are you *planning ahead* to remove from your life those things that will cause you to spend more time than you should dwelling on him?

If you are not stumbling because of something in your life, it may not be necessary for you to remove it. But if the relationship was characterized by a particular sin (sexual immorality, dishonesty, sinful anger), there may be wisdom in removing reminders, even if you're not stumbling, so that you won't be tempted to consider returning to your ex before such issues are corrected. "As a dog returns to his own vomit, so a fool repeats his folly" (Prov. 26:11).

Below is a checklist of things that you may want to remove from sight, return, give to someone else, throw away, or eliminate from your life.

- ☐ Unnecessary time communicating with your ex
- ☐ Gifts given to you by your ex
- ☐ Photographs of your ex
- ☐ Photographs taken by your ex
- ☐ Souvenirs of things that you and your ex did together
- ☐ Letters, notes, and cards that express your ex's affection for you
- ☐ Personal belongings of your ex that she may have loaned you
- ☐ Music that reminds you of your ex

Now let's consider those reminders of the past that are not so easily removed.[2] There are two extremes that should be avoided. At one end, take care not to become so paralyzed by the thought of being in the presence of anything that reminds you of your ex that you avoid going places and doing things that are clearly God's will for you. On the other hand, we should be careful to avoid those situations that we know from experience will tempt us to sin.

I've known some individuals who were so afraid of running into their ex (or people and things that reminded them of their ex) that they would actually avoid going to church. Think about that. Some people are so afraid of facing reminders of the past that they neglect to publicly worship the God who sustains them every moment of every day. Such people often don't realize the extent to which fear has crippled them. Neither do they consider that their fear may be an indication of how little they love the Lord.

If you are so afraid of something that you do not fulfill your biblical responsibility, you have been overcome by fear. To the extent that your fear keeps you from obeying God, your love for God is imperfect. "There is no fear in love; but perfect love casts out fear" (1 John 4:18). Your love for God and your confidence that He loves you ought to overcome your fear. If it doesn't, your love for Him is deficient. To love God, you must choose to obey Him whether or not you have a fearful experience. Loving Him means choosing to do those things He wants you to do. It means going to those places He wants you to go even if you are faced with things that remind you of your breakup. You may have to tell yourself, "If I have a fearful experience, I'll just have to have it. I'm not going to allow my fear to keep me from doing what God wants me to do—or from going where He wants me to go. If I am reminded of the past or encounter some other painful situation, I will trust the Lord to see me through it."

What have you been avoiding for fear of being reminded of the past?

- ☐ Church activities
- ☐ Fellowship with other Christians
- ☐ Ministry opportunities
- ☐ Family gatherings
- ☐ Social functions
- ☐ Household responsibilities
- ☐ Work-related activities
- ☐ Friendships

Decide today to love God more than you have been. Remove those reminders that cause you to stumble into sin, and face without fear those reminders that cannot or should not be removed.

17

Will I Still Love You Tomorrow?

Therefore do not worry about tomorrow, for tomorrow will worry about its own things. Sufficient for the day is its own trouble. —Matthew 6:34

What have you been worried about lately?

- ☐ Losing security
- ☐ Losing respect
- ☐ Losing money
- ☐ Losing your reputation
- ☐ Facing life without a companion
- ☐ Being treated as a second-class citizen
- ☐ Being a single parent
- ☐ Being abandoned by your friends
- ☐ Being lonely
- ☐ Having to make changes
- ☐ Not having all the resources you need

When a breakup occurs, there is great potential for anxiety—especially on the part of the one who didn't want things to end. But worry is a sin.

God forbids worry.

The Holy Spirit commands us in Philippians 4:6 to "be anxious for nothing." Jesus said in Matthew 6:34, "Do not worry about tomorrow."

Worry shows a lack of faith in God.

And why are you worried about clothing? Observe how the lilies of the field grow; they do not toil nor do they spin, yet I say to you that not even Solomon in all his glory clothed himself like one of these. But if God so clothes the grass of the field, which is alive today and tomorrow is thrown into the furnace, will He not much more clothe you? You of *little faith*! (Matt. 6:28–30 NASB)

Worry damages the body.

Do you not know that you are the temple of God and that the Spirit of God dwells in you? If anyone defiles the temple of God, God will destroy him. For the temple of God is holy, which temple you are. (1 Cor. 3:16–17)

Worry is known to cause such physiological effects as upset stomach, fatigue, diarrhea, high blood pressure, hives, hormonal changes, ulcers, irregularities and palpitations of the heart, and even heart attacks.

Worry wastes valuable time.

We are commanded to "walk circumspectly, not as fools but as wise, redeeming the time, because the days are evil" (Eph. 5:15–16). Worrying consumes an inordinate amount of time that could be better spent thinking about and doing those things that are eternally profitable.

What Is Worry?

Worrying is not the same as exercising foresight, preparing for the future, making plans, or taking appropriate precautions. All of these activities are biblically legitimate activities.

What, then, is worry?

Worry is a good emotion (*concern*) focused on the wrong day.[1]

> So do not worry about tomorrow; for tomorrow will care for itself. Each day has enough trouble of its own. (Matt. 6:34 NASB)

It is one thing to be concerned about the results of your broken relationship. It is quite another to be worried about how these concerns may adversely affect you at some point in the future. It's fine to determine how you are going to deal with your concerns or to develop a God-honoring plan to keep potential adversity from happening. It's wrong to anxiously focus your attention today on what may go wrong in the future, as though the Lord were not going to provide for or protect you.

Worry is experiencing unnecessary distress in the face of imaginary suffering.

Worry is fear in the absence of actual danger. It is overestimating the possibility of danger and magnifying the degree of potential adversity. Worry is often accompanied by imaginary pessimistic and foreboding outcomes that have been distorted beyond all likelihood.

One of the most common manifestations of this kind of worry is what I call *false prophecies*:

- I just know I'm going to have a panic attack if I see my ex at the restaurant.

- I will be scarred for the rest of my life because of this.
- Nobody's going to want to marry me when they find out.
- I'll never convince anyone to go out with me.
- I'll never be able to handle the responsibilities of being a single parent.
- I'll never get over losing him.
- I'll never be able to love somebody else the way I loved her.
- I'll go crazy if I have to spend the rest of my life by myself.
- I just know I'm going to die an old maid.

As I sometimes remind my counselees, "You're not a prophet, so stop making prophecies. If you're going to speculate about the future, you ought to do so with hope."

Worry is anticipating future suffering without anticipating the grace that God has promised to those who suffer.

Worry is thinking about your future as though God would not be there to take care of you. One of the most common manifestations of this kind of worry is what I refer to as *despairing prophecies:*[2]

- I could never face anything like that.
- I would be devastated if . . .
- I would just die if . . .
- I wouldn't be able to handle anything like that.
- I would be shattered if . . .
- That would be a disaster.
- That would be unbearable.
- That would be the most awful, horrible, terrible, unbearable, tragic, catastrophic calamity that could ever happen to me!

There was something in Paul's life that caused him considerable distress and for which he prayed three times that God would remove. God said no. So rather than worrying about how this "thorn in the flesh" was going to adversely affect him, he relied on God to provide him with all the grace he would ever need to see him through it. Paul even boasted about how God would be glorified through his infirmities rather than fretting about how they would mess up his future.

> Concerning this thing I pleaded with the Lord three times that it might depart from me. And He said to me, "My grace is sufficient for you, for My strength is made perfect in weakness." Therefore most gladly I will rather boast in my infirmities, that the power of Christ may rest upon me. (2 Cor. 12:8–9)

Worry is the by-product of an undisciplined mind.

> For God has not given us a spirit of fear, but of power and of love and of a sound mind. (2 Tim. 1:7)

The Greek term for *sound mind* in this passage has to do with self-control—especially in one's thoughts, decisions, and judgments. The term may be rendered as "to have right thoughts about what one should do" or "to let one's mind guide one's body."[3] You can defeat fear by learning how to control your thoughts. Take a moment to identify your greatest worries—especially those that have been spawned as a result of your breakup.

WHAT DO I WORRY ABOUT MOST?

List those things about which you've been most anxious. Begin with your most recent anxieties.

1. _____

2. _____

3. _____

4. _____

5. _____

6. _____

7. _____

18

I Say a Little Prayer and Supplication with Thanksgiving

Be anxious for nothing, but in everything by prayer and supplication, with thanksgiving, let your requests be made known to God; and the peace of God, which surpasses all understanding, will guard your hearts and minds through Christ Jesus. Finally, brethren, whatever things are true, whatever things are noble, whatever things are just, whatever things are pure, whatever things are lovely, whatever things are of good report, if there is any virtue and if there is anything praiseworthy—meditate on these things. The things which you learned and received and heard and saw in me, these do, and the God of peace will be with you. —Philippians 4:6–9

You are about to come face-to-face with a powerful, state-of-the-art treatment for worry. I believe it to be more effective in the long run, safer, and in many cases faster-acting than any anti-anxiety medication on the market. It is prescribed in the fourth chapter of Philippians. There are three stages to this treatment. The first is biblical praying (verses 6 and 7).

> Be anxious for nothing, but in everything by prayer and supplication, with thanksgiving, let your requests be made known to God; and the peace of God, which surpasses all understanding, will guard your hearts and minds through Christ Jesus.

This is not your run-of-the-mill kind of prayer—it is highly specialized. In fact, Paul uses three different words for *prayer* in this prescription. They are *prayer*, *supplication*, and *requests*. *Prayer* is the most frequently used New Testament word for this activity. *Supplication* is a more specific term for prayer about something one urgently needs. *Requests* has to do with the details pertaining to one's supplication.

This prayer contains one of the key ingredients for conquering worry. It's the phrase "with thanksgiving." Your prayers must not simply contain petitions for what you need or want—they must also include expressions of thankfulness to God.

I'd like to suggest three areas of thanksgiving—or perhaps it's better to say three tenses of thanksgiving.

1. *The Past.* For what can I thank God concerning previous answers to similar prayers?
2. *The Present.* What is there in these present circumstances for which I can thank Him?
3. *The Future.* How can I thank Him for what He might be doing in the future?

Biblical Thinking

The second step of our anti-anxiety treatment is biblical thinking. Take a look at verse 8. "Finally, brethren, whatever things are true, whatever things are noble, whatever things are just, whatever things are pure, whatever things are lovely, whatever things are of good report, if there is any virtue and if there is anything praiseworthy—meditate on these things."

To knock out despair, you must change your thought patterns. To turn down those intensely disturbing feelings, you must change your thought patterns. To overcome grief, resentment, and depression, you must change the way you think. To overcome fear and worry, you will have to discipline your mind. You will have to change your anxious thoughts to thoughts that reflect biblical hope. You will have to replace thoughts that are theologically inaccurate with ones that are accurate—especially when it comes to how you think about God. Your thoughts about the future that do not conform to reality must be replaced with "whatever things are true" (i.e., things that conform to reality).

Let's take a few of those false prophecies we looked at in the last chapter.

"I just know I'm going to have a panic attack if I see my ex at the restaurant."

Wouldn't it be more biblical to think something like this? "The Lord will give me the grace to respond appropriately to my ex if I see him at the restaurant." Or perhaps this might be appropriate: "If I have a 'panic attack,' I'll just have to have one. This is Mom and Dad's anniversary dinner, and I'm not going to selfishly allow my fear of meeting my ex to keep me from honoring my parents."

"I will be scarred for the rest of my life because of this."

Isn't this a better way to phrase it? "I know it might be difficult, but God is able to use this embarrassing circumstance as a means of giving me His sufficient grace. The Bible says in several places (Prov. 3:34; James 4:6; 1 Peter 5:5), 'God gives grace to the humble.'" Or how about, "I've given my reputation to God. He is able to give 'beauty for ashes' (Isa. 61:3) and 'restore the years that the swarming locust has eaten'" (Joel 2:25).

"I'll never get over losing him."

How's this for a biblical alternative? "Getting over losing him is not as important to God as getting over and losing my anxiety problem." Or maybe you'll find this one a better fit: "*Never* is a long time. I'm confident that God will cause my grief to go away if I respond biblically to losing him."

"I'll go crazy if I have to spend the rest of my life by myself."

Wouldn't it be more accurate to think, "I'm more likely to go crazy if I don't learn how to get my anxiety under control. To live the rest of my life by myself is not a sin. To make an idol out of being married is." Or how about this angle? "I'd rather want what I don't have than have what I don't want—a marriage that is not God's best for me."

The possibilities are really endless. When it comes to rearranging your thought patterns, there truly is "more than one way to skin a cat." The more you can include Scripture in your amended thought patterns, the more potent your spiritual tranquilizer will be. If practiced consistently, the process of changing your thoughts from anxiety-oriented propositions to thoughts containing biblical truth should produce remarkable results in a relatively short period of time.

Biblical Action

If you want to conquer anxiety, it's not enough to simply pray and meditate. As Paul explains in Philippians 4:9, you must *do* certain things as well. "The things which you learned and received and heard and saw in me, these do, and the God of peace will be with you."

I'm going to suggest two categories of biblical actions that are helpful in knocking out anxiety. The first has to do with the anxiety itself. Any *direct* biblical action you can take that will help prevent what you are worried about from occurring will qualify. The question to ask yourself is, "What can I *do* (what actions can I take today) to keep what I'm worried about from happening tomorrow?" These actions include such things as studying what the Bible says about your particular concern, getting godly counsel, or formulating a biblical plan of action to solve the potential problem.

Rather than worrying about how you are going to cut down the entire forest, try to determine how may trees the Lord would want you to chop down today. Tomorrow is another day with another section of trees to cut. "Do not worry about tomorrow; for tomorrow will care for itself. Each day has enough trouble of its own" (Matt. 6:34 NASB). If each day you prayerfully plan to ax a limited number of trees, you will find it possible to address your concerns without worry. You may even discover that the Lord has been on the other side of the forest bulldozing trees down much faster than you ever could.

The second kind of action you can take to thwart worry has to do with getting your mind off your worries and onto more profitable things. Is there any biblical action you can take that will *indirectly* help by temporarily replacing anxious thoughts with thoughts that are more God-honoring and productive? How can you engage your mind with wholesome activities such as fulfilling your daily responsibilities, reading a good book, listening to uplifting music? Even a game of tennis or golf could force you to think about something more pleasing to God than your worry.

To help you become more proficient in using this anti-anxiety treatment, you may want to start an anxiety journal. This is a worksheet on which you can work out your anxieties in written form according to Philippians 4:6–9.

1. Photocopy as many journal pages as you think you'll need in a given two-week period. If all goes well, the frequency of your anxieties will diminish, so you'll use fewer copies in subsequent weeks.

2. At the top of each sheet, underneath the words "My Anxiety (what I am concerned about)," describe the exact nature of your anxiety.

3. Underneath the words "Biblical Prayer," write out your personal prayer. Be as specific as possible with your requests. Most importantly, express thankfulness to God for as many things as you can—especially those things that are connected to your concern. (Remember to *thank* in terms of past, present, and future.)

4. Underneath the words "Biblical Thoughts," write out how you are going to think about your concern so as not to worry. Reconstruct your thought patterns to reflect biblical hope and theological accuracy—especially when it comes to trusting in God's sovereignty and goodness and His other fatherly attributes. Use Philippians 4:8 as a guideline. Your reconstructed thoughts do not have to be a verbatim quotation from Scripture. A personalized application of a biblical principle or directive will do nicely. Write down the appropriate Scripture references next to each thought for future study, meditation, and/or memorization.

5. Underneath the words "Biblical Actions," write out each specific action you can take that will either address each concern on a day-by-day basis or focus your mind on more noble matters. The two questions to ask yourself are: "What can I *do* (what actions can I take today) to keep what I'm worried about from happening tomorrow?" and "What can I *do* (what actions can I take at this moment) that will engage my mind with more profitable thoughts than worry?"

ANXIETY JOURNAL

My Anxiety (what I am concerned about):

_____

_____

Biblical Prayer:

_____

_____

_____

_____

Biblical Thoughts:

☐ _____

_____

☐ _____

_____

☐ _____

_____

Biblical Actions:

☐ _____

_____

☐ _____

_____

☐ _____

_____

19

I'm Nobody Till
Somebody Loves Me

*Let nothing be done through selfish ambition or conceit,
but in lowliness of mind let each esteem others better
than himself. —Philippians 2:3*

M y self-esteem has been at an all-time low ever since the
breakup. I'll never be the same again because of all the hurt
Fred has caused me. My feelings of inferiority have turned me
into an emotional basket case. I've got to learn how to improve
my poor self-image and feel good about myself again so I can get
over this mess and get on with my life. I know I'll never be able
to grow as a Christian until I overcome my self-esteem issues."

Thoughts such as this are common today—even among Christians. It's little wonder. Even Christian books, magazines, radio,
television, and video programs (not to mention pulpits) are promoting certain ideas about self-image that are not taught in Scripture.
The idea that "self-esteem" is essential for one's happiness ought

to throw up a red flag in the mind of the discerning believer who understands the implications of Philippians 2:3. Our happiness is not related as much to how we esteem ourselves as it is to how we esteem others. Christians have been inundated with humanistic presuppositions that they believe to be theologically sound.

Allow me to briefly point out a few of the fallacies implicit in that first paragraph.

1. There is a part of man's nonmaterial being (such as his mind, conscience, or will) called a "self-image" (cf. 1 Cor. 2:13).
2. Inferiority is a feeling rather than a judgment or self-evaluation (cf. Rom. 2:14–15).
3. People are victims of something beyond their control (cf. Gen. 3:12–13).
4. A good self-image is a prerequisite to success and happiness (Josh. 1:8).
5. God's ability to help people change is dependent on one's having a good self-image (cf. Rom. 8:29).

The construct of self-image doesn't exist in the Bible.[1] The Scriptures speak of man's heart, his mind, his conscience, his emotions, his thoughts, and his motives, but say nothing about self-image. We are mistaken when we view self-image as an entity in and of itself. It is not an organ of the soul that can be squashed, flattened, punctured, inflated, deflated, damaged, or devastated. It can't be isolated, and fixed, or modified—at least not directly.

"What do you mean by 'not directly'?"

To answer that question, we must first look at and interpret the idea of self-image "not in words which man's wisdom teaches but which the Holy Spirit teaches, comparing spiritual things with spiritual" (1 Cor. 2:13). Self-image can best be classified as a judgment one makes as he evaluates himself. You and I conme

tinually make judgments about ourselves in a variety of areas (cf. 1 Cor. 2:15–16; 11:31; Titus 3:11).

- How likable am I?
- Where am I failing?
- How successful am I?
- Where am I excelling?
- Am I growing in Christ?
- How do I relate to others?
- What are my talents and gifts?
- Am I fulfilling my responsibilities?
- What are my strengths and weaknesses?
- Is the way I'm living my life pleasing to God?

The answers to these questions form our self-evaluation. This internal evaluation is what is commonly referred to as our self-image. Self-image, therefore, is not an emotion or a feeling, but rather a part of our cognitive process. It is fundamentally thought—not feeling.

We may feel good about our self-evaluation, or we may feel bad about it. But the feelings are the result of our thoughts.

People don't actually "feel inferior." Rather, they judge themselves to be inferior and feel lousy about their self-evaluation. These inferiority judgments are at the root of all so-called self-image problems. As a Christian, you should have as your objective not to have a "good" or "positive" self-image, but rather to have an accurate self-image based on biblically correct perceptions and evaluations.

Our self-evaluations tend to fall into one or more of three separate categories.

THREE CATEGORIES OF INFERIORITY JUDGMENTS

INACCURATE PERCEPTIONS	ACCURATE BUT NOT SINFUL	ACCURATE AND SINFUL
Change in **Perceptions**	Change in **Values**	Change in **Behavior**

The first classification has to do with the accuracy of our own perceptions. The effects of sin on our minds hinder us from interpreting life from God's point of view. That's one reason we're so dependent on the Bible for perspective. What's more, our sinful hearts are capable of seriously distorting our judgments. Self-evaluations are often wrong. A person whose inferiority judgments are the result of inaccurate self-perceptions must learn how to change those perceptions, primarily with the assistance of Scripture and secondarily with the assistance of wise (objective) and trusted friends.

The second kind of inferiority judgment has to do with a conscience and/or value system that has not been programmed biblically. Sometimes we judge ourselves to be inadequate in a particular area in which the Bible does not require adequacy. I can't fly an airplane, or quilt, or box. But I don't consider myself to be an inadequate person, because God doesn't say I'm supposed to do any of those things. Since it's not a sin for me to not be a pilot or a quilter or a boxer, I don't judge myself to be deficient even though in those areas I'm significantly inferior to others.

If I judge myself to be an inadequate person or deficient in character as a result of these inferiorities, there is something askew with my value system. Either I'm overvaluing something that God doesn't value or I'm not valuing as much as I should something He values very highly. I may even be doing both. The person who says to himself, "I will be miserable if I'm not in a romantic relationship" or "I'm a nobody when nobody loves me" may be overvaluing (making an idol out of) the blessedness of marriage or undervaluing the blessedness of serving the Lord without distraction. A person whose inferiority judgments are the result of accurate self-perceptions concerning things about which it is not sinful to be inferior must learn how to change his values.

The third category of inferiority judgment involves accurate perceptions of sinful behavior patterns that have not yet been corrected. It doesn't matter how effectively you are able to change your perceptions and your values by preaching the gospel to yourself or internalizing "positional truth" about your relationship with your heavenly Father through Christ the Son. If you don't in some way begin correcting those sinful thoughts, motives, patterns of speech, habits, and attitudes (if you don't actively cooperate with the Holy Spirit's sanctifying presence in your life), you will continue to be plagued by inferiority judgments and feel miserable about yourself. Therefore, a person whose inferiority judgments are the result of accurate self-perceptions about the sinful patterns in his life must learn how to change his behavior.

What's the condition of your self-image? How has your former relationship affected your self-perceptions? Are you lying to yourself about who you are? Have you internalized any wrong values as a result of that relationship? Have you picked up any bad habits as a result of the relationship (or not worked hard enough on correcting the ones you had before the relationship began)?

If you are interested in acquiring a biblically accurate self-image, consider the following exercise. Make a list of your inferiorities. Prayerfully ask yourself, "What are those areas of my life in which I judge myself to be inadequate?" Once the list is complete, see if you can put each inferiority judgment into at least one of the three categories above. Then, in dependence on God's Spirit, and perhaps with the help of a wise pastor or counselor, get to work on making those changes.[2]

20

Misheard It through the Grapevine?

A righteous man will be remembered forever. He will have no fear of bad news; his heart is steadfast, trusting in the LORD.
—*Psalm 112:6–7* NIV

"I don't feel the same way about you as I used to."

"I think we need to start seeing other people."

"It's over! I'm never coming back to you!"

"Reconciliation is out of the question. You need to get on with your life and forget about me."

"A friend of mine met your ex at the supermarket last night, and she was trashing you big-time."

"I heard your ex is going to bring his new girl to the game."

"Did you hear who your ex was seen with?"

"It looks like your ex is going to be getting married soon."

"The deposition for your divorce proceeding is scheduled for the twenty-third."

"The judge signed the papers this morning. Here they are. Congratulations! You're now a free man."

"Mom, I met Daddy's new girlfriend this weekend. She seems really nice."

For those who go through the breakup of a romantic relationship, bad news often continues to come after the separation takes place. How do you respond when bad news comes your way? Do you live in constant apprehension of running into your ex, of seeing old friends, of going to the mailbox, or of getting that dreaded telephone call? Are you paralyzed by fear? Or, like the lyricist of Psalm 112, is your heart steadfast, trusting in the Lord?

His ability to not be afraid of bad news had to do with the fact that his heart was fixed—not only in the sense of being repaired, but like a laser-guided missile that is not easily diverted from its course once it locks onto its target. To be fixed is to be steadfast and unmovable.

The Hebrew word for "fixed" or "steadfast" in Psalm 112:7 may also be translated *prepared.* In expounding on our text, Charles Spurgeon provides several examples of what it means to have a heart that is both fixed and prepared for bad news, as it trusts in the Lord.

The Christian's heart is fixed as to duty. He says within himself, "It is my business so to walk as Christ also walked: it can never be right for me to do contrary to God's will, I have set the Lord always before me, and in integrity of heart will I walk all my way, wherever that way may lead." Such a man is prepared for anything. Whatever trial comes, he is prepared to meet it, because his soul is resolved that come gain, come loss, he will not be dishonest to make himself rich; he will not tell a lie to win a kingdom, he will not give up a principle to save his life.

But, more comfortable than this, the Christian's heart is fixed as to knowledge, and so prepared. There are some things which a believer knows and is quite fixed about. He knows, for instance, that God sits in the stern of the vessel when it rocks the most. He believes that an invisible hand is always on the world's tiller,[1] and that wherever providence may drift, Jehovah steers it. That reassuring knowledge prepares him for everything. "It is my Father's will," he thinks. He looks over the raging waters, and he sees the spirit of Jesus treading the billows, and he hears a voice which says, "It is I, be not afraid." He knows too that God is always wise, and knowing this, he is prepared for all events. They cannot come amiss, he thinks, there can be no accidents, no mistakes, nothing can occur which ought not to occur. If I should lose all I have, it is better that I should lose than have, if God so wills: the worst calamity is the wisest and the kindest thing that could occur to me if God ordains it. "We know that all things work together for good to them that love God." The Christian does not merely hold this as a theory, but he knows it as a matter of fact. Everything has worked for good as yet; the poisonous drugs that have been mixed in the compound have nevertheless worked the cure; the sharp cuts of the lancet have cleansed out the proud flesh and facilitated the healing. Every event as yet has worked out the most divinely blessed results; and so, believing this, that God rules it, that God rules wisely, that God brings good out of evil, the believer's heart is fixed and he is well prepared.

Let me remind you of one form of fixedness which will make you outride every storm, namely, fixedness as to eternal things. "I cannot lose"—the Christian may say—"I cannot lose my best things." When a carrier has many parcels to carry, if he has gold and silver or precious stones, he is sure to put them near himself. Perhaps he has some common goods, and these he ties on behind: some thief, it is possible, steals from the cart some of the common goods which were outside. "Oh, well," says the man when he gets home, "I am sorry to lose anything, but my precious things are all right; they are all safe; I thank God the thief could not run away with them." Now, our earthly goods and even our dearest friends are only the common mercies of God, but our Savior, our God, our eternal interest in the covenant, our heaven which we are soon to inherit, these are kept where they cannot be lost. If adversity should come and take everything else away, yet, Christian, your heart is still fixed because you have a grasp of eternal things; and neither life, nor death, nor time, nor eternity, can make you let go your hold of the glory which is to be revealed in you. Thus you are prepared, come what may.

I will add only one more thought to this point: I believe that holy gratitude is one blessed way of fixing the soul on God and preparing it for trouble. When I think of what our God has done for us, how he saved us from going down into the pit and found a ransom in his own dear Son, when we remember how he has plucked us out of the horrible pit and out of the miry clay, let him do what seems good to Him: the Lord gave us Christ, then let Him take away what He will, we cannot think harshly of Him; after such a proof of love, we are bound to Him by such ties of gratitude that should He take away one mercy after the other, till there is hardly one left, we will yet bless His name. "Though He slay me, yet will I trust in Him." Let every saint of God feel himself so fixed and bound by ties of gratitude that he is prepared, whatever may come, still to bless his God.[2]

The next time bad news comes, will you continue to walk in obedience to God? Will you believe that God is sovereign, causing all things to work together for your good? Will you keep your focus on eternal things rather than grieving over the potential loss of some cherished pleasure? Will you be thankful for what the Lord has already given you—eternal life and all the blessings and privileges that come from being a child of God?

Now, before we proceed to the next chapter, I must say a final word about another form of bad news: those unsubstantiated prophetic speculations that your ex (or other persons) may have made concerning what will happen in the future. Have you set your heart on such speculative babble, believing that the person who uttered them has spoken ex cathedra (with the same authority as if they were proclaimed from the throne of God)?

Why? The Bible condemns all those who make plans about the future without considering God's will in the matter.

> Come now, you who say, "Today or tomorrow we will go to such and such a city, and spend a year there and engage in business and make a profit." Yet you do not know what your life will be like tomorrow. You are just a vapor that appears for a little while and then vanishes away. Instead, you ought to say, "If the Lord wills, we will live and also do this or that." But as it is, you boast in your arrogance; all such boasting is evil. (James 4:13-16 NASB)

It is wrong for others to make prophecies about the future that clearly go against Scripture. Guard your heart from accepting as an inevitable reality any prophetic type of utterance about the future made by any person who does not consult the Scriptures in his or her daily decisions.

21

Won't Look Back

I strive always to keep my conscience clear before God and man. —Acts 24:16 NIV

Be forewarned. This is probably *not* going to be a feel-good chapter—at least not initially. What you are about to read is contrary to what you may have heard or read elsewhere about getting over a broken relationship and getting on with your life. "Just put it behind you, don't look back, forget about him/her" is the popular advice. While appearing to be reminiscent of Philippians 3:13 ("forgetting¹ those things which are behind and reaching forward to those things which are ahead"), such advice customarily neglects a significant biblical doctrine: the necessity of maintaining a clear conscience.

Yes, one of your goals is to put the past behind you. It is also important that you not focus on certain things from the past. But the "don't look back" part of the equation is something that has caused a lot of people trouble. There *is* one area of your relationship to which you will have to look back if you want to truly forget the past and face the future with confidence—past offenses you've committed against your ex for which you've not yet asked forgiveness.

The apostle Paul had a lot to say about his own conscience being clear (Acts 24;16; 1 Cor. 4:4; 2 Cor. 1:12; 2 Tim. 1:3). He informed Timothy twice in the same letter about the dangers associated with having a conscience that is not clear.

> Now the purpose of the commandment is love from a pure heart, from *a good conscience*, and from sincere faith, from which some, having strayed, have *turned aside* to idle talk, desiring to be teachers of the law, understanding neither what they say nor the things which they affirm. (1 Tim. 1:5–7)

> This charge I commit to you, son Timothy, according to the prophecies previously made concerning you, that by them you may wage the good warfare, having faith and *a good conscience*, which some having rejected, concerning the faith have *suffered shipwreck*, of whom are Hymenaeus and Alexander, whom I *delivered to Satan* that they may learn not to blaspheme. (1 Tim. 1:18–20)

Our conscience is an amazing thing. When we sin (or even think we might have sinned), our conscience triggers an unpleasant emotion that we call guilt. Our conscience, when functioning properly,[2] does not allow us to easily forget the past. The lack of a clear conscience impacts our future in a variety of ways. In addition to distorting our theology (1 Tim. 1:5–7) and shipwrecking our faith (1 Tim. 1:18–20), it can also produce irrational fears (cf. Prov. 28:1).

There are more reasons to clear your conscience than simply eliminating guilt. For one thing, when you are made aware that you have sinned against another, God commands you to "leave your gift there before the altar, and go your way . . . [to] be reconciled to your brother" (Matt. 5:24). For another, you will receive a special blessing for doing so. Admittedly, the process of asking for forgiveness is a humbling one. But God has promised that He "gives grace to the humble" (Prov. 3:34; James 4:6; 1 Peter 5:5). "Grace" in these passages does not refer to the unmerited favor of God as much as it does the supernatural power of God.

Because of your breakup, you are in special need of the enabling power that God's Spirit can provide. The humility that you will likely experience as a result of clearing your conscience with your ex (and anyone else you may have offended) will put you in the position to receive more of what you need to properly "fall out of love."

When people come to me for counseling after having gone through the breakup of a romantic relationship, I typically have them do three things.

Make a list of the specific ways in which you have sinned against your ex.

I have included at the back of this book (Appendix D) a checklist to help you evaluate those areas in which you may need to confess to and ask forgiveness from your ex. Prayerfully review this list from his point of view. Try to imagine how your sin might have hurt or offended him. As you think of additional items to place on the list, be sure to identify your sins by their biblical names (selfishness, impatience, bitterness, pride, etc.).

Confess those sins to your ex.

Determine the appropriate method of approach (telephone call, face-to-face, or letter). Discretion must be used in determining not only the appropriate means of asking for forgiveness but also whether or not contact with your ex will cause more harm than good. In some cases (e.g., if your ex is now married to someone who would not appreciate your contact), it would be better to confess your sins only to God and prayerfully wait for a more discreet time to make things right. By making the list and preparing your heart for such an occasion, your conscience should be greatly relieved, even if you never have the opportunity to officially ask for forgiveness. In such cases, it may be a greater demonstration of your love to bear the burden yourself than to place your ex in an uncomfortable position.

Ask for forgiveness.

Take a moment to read the following excerpt on forgiveness from *The Heart of Anger.*

What Does It Mean to Forgive?

As Christians, we are commanded to forgive "just as God in Christ also has forgiven you" (Eph. 4:32). What does that mean? God says, "I, even I, am the one who wipes out your transgressions for My own sake; and I will *not remember* your sins" and "I will forgive their iniquity, and their sin I will *remember no more*" (Isa. 43:25, Jer. 31:34)

So, does God have amnesia? Certainly not! God is omniscient (all knowing) and knew about your sins even before you committed them. When the Bible speaks of God forgetting our sins, it refers to the fact that when God has truly forgiven a person, He does not hold them against the forgiven sinner. He doesn't charge them to our account. Rather, God will charge them to the account of the Lord Jesus Christ, who died on the cross to pay the price of the penalty of guilty sinners like you and me. Christ's death was a substitution. He died to take the punishment for our sin so that we, as saved individuals, might be credited with His righteousness. When we truly believe the gospel, God promises to not hold our sins against us. Instead, He imputes the perfect righteousness of His Son to our account. What is the gospel (or good news)? The gospel is simply this: If we repent and place our faith in what Christ has done by substituting Himself for us on the cross and rising from the dead, God promises to forgive all our sins and give us eternal life.

Forgiveness, therefore, is first and foremost a *promise.* As God promised not to hold the sins of repentant sinners against them, so we also must promise not to hold the sins of those we've forgiven against them. You may demonstrate this promise by *not* doing at least *three* things to the person you've forgiven. First, you may not bring up the forgiven offense to the forgiven person so as to use it against him/her. Second, you may not discuss the forgiven offense with others. Finally, you may not dwell on the forgiven offense yourself but rather remind yourself that you have forgiven your offender, "just as God in Christ also has forgiven you."[3]

When you ask for forgiveness from your ex, you are attempting to secure for yourself these three promises. You are trying to tie up any loose ends by having him commit to not holding your offense against you ever again. In light of this, I'd like to suggest an effective approach.

Acknowledge the fact that you have sinned.

Let your ex know that you realize what you did was wrong. *Example*: "I was wrong for not admitting when I was wrong while we were courting/married."

Identify your specific sin by its biblical name.

Using biblical terminology, let your ex know that you now realize your sin was a violation of God's Word and therefore a sin against Him. *Example*: "It was my own *pride* and *selfishness* that kept me from acknowledging my faults and sins."

Acknowledge the harm that your offense caused your ex.

Show remorse (sympathy) for the hurt that your sin has caused. *Example*: "I really am sorry for how my sin exasperated you and hindered our ability to resolve conflicts."

Ask for forgiveness.

This step puts the ball in your ex's court. It is your attempt not only to reconcile with your offended brother and clear your conscience, but also to secure for yourself the three promises of forgiveness. *Example*: "Will you forgive me?"

Some people still experience guilt even after clearing their consciences. Although there are several explanations for this phenomenon (such as not being a Christian, worry, or faulty theology), one of the most common has to do with certain habit patterns in one's life that have not yet been changed. A biblically programmed conscience will not allow you to easily forget those sins in your past that have not been confessed *and forsaken*. "He who covers his sins will not prosper, but whoever confesses *and forsakes* them will have mercy" (Prov. 28:13). Sometimes a Christian can experience guilt even after confession of sin because he knows that in all likelihood he is going to repeat the sin in the future. He knows he is still bound by the sin that has overtaken him. What such a person may be experiencing is genuine guilt over being bound by the habit that generated the sin for which he has asked forgiveness. It is not until he experiences a change of habit that his conscience will be thoroughly cleared. Before we can truly forget our past sins, we must forsake them.

Was your contribution to the breakdown of this relationship the fact that you have a short temper? The more you learn to control your temper, the less guilty you will feel. Perhaps it was selfishness that kept you from giving your ex what she really needed. The more you learn to be a giver rather than a taker, the more confidence you will have that history will not repeat itself. The realization that Christ has changed your life will give you boldness to face the future with the confidence that the sins of your past are truly in the past and that your conscience is clear both *legally* and *experientially*.

22

It's Your Party

So he said, "I have been very zealous for the LORD God of hosts; for the children of Israel have forsaken Your covenant, torn down Your altars, and killed Your prophets with the sword. I alone am left; and they seek to take my life."
—*1 Kings 19:10*

Feeling sorry for yourself will prolong your misery and hinder your ability to get over the broken relationship. It may also repulse some of your friends. Here's a sampling of what self-pity sounds like in an individual who is struggling with such a breakup.

- I'll never be able to enjoy a loving relationship.
- Why do I have to be so unhappy?
- Why did I have to be the one to get dumped?
- Why did the Lord allow such a hurtful thing to happen to me?

- All I ever wanted in life was to have a family. Why can't God let me have such a good thing?
- I hate my life.
- You have no idea how difficult it is to go through something like this.
- Nobody understands how hard this is for me.
- I wish everybody would just leave me alone.
- (Two weeks later) Nobody ever calls me. Why doesn't anybody care about me?
- None of my friends know how to help or encourage me— they all have husbands or boyfriends.
- What's the use of trying to live the Christian life? It's too much trouble and will never pay enough dividends—at least not in this life.
- I wish I could run away to a place where nobody knows me.
- I wish I'd never been born.

People who are throwing pity parties for themselves often use sweeping generalizations or exaggerations (*nobody*, *everyone*, *never*, *ever*, *always*, *only*, etc.). Elijah said, "I am the only one left" (1 Kings 19:10, 14 NIV). Asaph said of the wicked:

> They have no struggles,
>   their bodies are healthy and strong.
> They are free from the burdens common to man;
>   they are not plagued by human ills.
> . . . .
> This is what the wicked are like—
>   always carefree. . . . (Ps. 73:4–5, 12 NIV)

He said to himself:

> All day long I have been plagued;
>   I have been punished every morning. (Ps. 73:14 NIV)

Jeremiah asked the Lord:

> Why is my pain unending
> and my wound grievous and incurable? (Jer. 15:18 NIV)

Job predicted:

> My eyes will never see happiness again. (Job 7:7 NIV)

We can learn a lot from Job, that blameless and upright man who feared God and eschewed evil (except for that momentary season in his life when he began feeling sorry for himself).

Perhaps the most obvious characteristic about self-pitying individuals is that they complain about their circumstances—often putting the worst possible interpretation on them.

> For the thing I greatly feared has come upon me,
> And what I dreaded has happened to me. (Job 3:25)

> I will not restrain my mouth;
> I will speak in the anguish of my spirit;
> I will complain in the bitterness of my soul. (Job 7:11 NASB)

> I will give free course to my complaint,
> I will speak in the bitterness of my soul. (Job 10:1)

> Even today my complaint is bitter;
> My hand is listless because of my groaning. (Job 23:2)

Philippians 2:14 describes half of the remedy to this problem: "Do all things without complaining and disputing." The other half of the solution is found in 1 Thessalonians 5:18: "In everything give thanks; for this is the will of God in Christ Jesus for you."

Most of Job's complaining was directed against God.

If I called and He answered me,
I would not believe that He was listening to my voice.
For He crushes me with a tempest,
And multiplies my wounds without cause.
He will not allow me to catch my breath,
But fills me with bitterness." (Job 9:16–17)

Does it seem good to You that You should oppress,
That You should despise the work of Your hands,
And smile on the counsel of the wicked? (Job 10:3)

Why then have You brought me out of the womb?
Oh, that I had perished and no eye had seen me!
    (Job 10:18)

As water wears away stones,
And as torrents wash away the soil of the earth;
So You destroy the hope of man. (Job 14:19)

Another indication of Job's anger at God is his defiant demand that God explain why He did certain things.

Have I sinned?
What have I done to You, O watcher of men?
Why have You set me as Your target,
So that I am a burden to myself? (Job 7:20)

Why then have You brought me out of the womb? (Job 10:18)

I love what Elihu says to Job as he chastens him for his angry attitude. "Why do you complain against Him that He does not give an account of all His doings?" (Job 33:13 NASB) God does not owe us an explanation for why He does what He does. He is God, and He can do what He pleases. And whatever He does will always be good.

But indeed, O man, who are you to reply against God? Will the thing formed say to him who formed it, "Why have you made me like this?" Does not the potter have power over the clay, from the same lump to make one vessel for honor and another for dishonor? (Rom. 9:20–21)

Even if you knew the answer to that perplexing *why* question, it may not help you as much as you might think. You may not like God's answer or agree with His reasoning. In time, God may see fit to show you why He allowed the breakup (or any other difficult circumstance that He has brought into your life). When you get to heaven, you'll certainly understand. But for now, perhaps the question you should be asking is not a *why* question, but rather a *what* question: "What does God want me to do about the problem He has brought into my life?"

Envy, Vain Regrets, and Unrealistic Expectations

Self-pitying people have a difficult time understanding why God allows others to have the things for which they long. They get angry because they perceive God to be blessing others who are no more righteous then they, while at the same time withholding those blessings from themselves. In chapter 21, Job discloses what appears to be a level of envy for the wicked that would make Asaph (Ps. 73) blush.[1] Here is a sampling (vv. 7–13):

Why do the wicked live and become old,
Yes, become mighty in power?
Their descendants are established with them in their sight,
And their offspring before their eyes.
Their houses are safe from fear,
Neither is the rod of God upon them.
Their bull breeds without failure;
Their cow calves without miscarriage.

They send forth their little ones like a flock,
And their children dance.
They sing to the tambourine and harp,
And rejoice to the sound of the flute.
They spend their days in wealth,
And in a moment go down to the grave.

The short answer to the problem of envying the wicked is to do what Asaph did. Go into the sanctuary of God (read the Bible), and understand that the apparent blessings of the wicked are only *apparent!*

Some self-pitying people struggle with the "I wish I'd never been born" regret. In Job 3:1, we read, "After this Job opened his mouth and cursed the day of his birth." The rest of the chapter is basically a continuation of this theme.

A milder variation of this self-pitying theme is the "What's the use in trying?" attitude. One of the best antidotes to this mind-set is to develop the outlook that the apostle Paul had about living and dying.

> For to me, to live is Christ and to die is gain. If I am to go on living in the body, this will mean fruitful labor for me. Yet what shall I choose? I do not know! I am torn between the two: I desire to depart and be with Christ, which is better by far; but it is more necessary for you that I remain in the body. (Phil. 1:21–24 NIV)

The great apostle lived life for Christ, not for himself. He focused his attention not on his troubles (of which he had many), but on serving God and His people.

Self-pitying people tend to expect others to be excessively loyal to them. Job seems to have expected his friends to side with him against God. "To him who is afflicted, kindness should be shown by his friend, even though he forsakes the fear of the Almighty" (Job 6:14).

146

Job hinted to his friends that they should be kind to him even if he were to forsake the Lord. Certainly friends should love at all times (Prov. 17:17), and some of Job's friends were unkind because of the way they accused him. But love in such cases is often best shown by biblical confrontation. "Faithful are the wounds of a friend" (Prov. 27:6). A true friend will be more loyal to the Lord and to the truth of His Word than he is to you.

Job's first three friends failed him by not identifying his problem biblically. But his fourth and youngest friend, Elihu, hit the bull's-eye. "Then the wrath of Elihu, the son of Barachel the Buzite, of the family of Ram, was aroused against Job; his wrath was aroused *because he justified himself rather than God*" (Job 32:2).

Self-pity is rooted in such things as selfishness, pride, idolatry, envy, and resentment. It tempts us to focus on what we don't have (selfishness), what we believe we deserve (pride), what we want (idolatry), what others have been given that we have not (envy), and why God has seen fit to bless others instead of us (resentment).

The book of Job was probably the first book of the Bible to be written. Consequently, Job didn't have the benefit of the Scriptures to help him overcome his sinful attitudes. God had to intervene and speak directly to him to make His point. Today, God speaks through the Bible, where He gives us everything we need to crash our pity party and get on with serving Him.

23

Who Can You Turn To?

Whom have I in heaven but You? And there is none upon earth that I desire besides You. My flesh and my heart fail; but God is the strength of my heart and my portion forever.
—Psalm 73:25–26

There is a special temptation into which you may be in danger of falling as a result of the breakup. That is the temptation to tranquilize your emotions with temporal things that are neither capable of satisfying your deepest longings nor able to provide anything but a temporary respite from your distress. The question to ask yourself is: "How do I spell relief?"

There are many options available today from which people may choose. To what or to whom have you been turning in an effort to tranquilize your hurting heart?

☐ **Alcohol and Drugs:** Alcohol is the most readily available substance of abuse. It comes in a variety of forms and flavors. Antianxiety medications and pain pills are among the most commonly prescribed and abused drugs in the United States.

☐ **Sexual Pleasure:** Masturbation and pornography may provide a fair amount of pleasure and a temporary distraction from stress and distress. But the guilt associated with these two addicting vices can be very debilitating.

☐ **Cigarettes:** These can be more addicting than most drugs and alcohol. They can cause serious damage to your body (the Holy Spirit's temple).

☐ **Television:** Too much of this will keep you from fulfilling your biblical responsibilities, pollute your mind with worldly values, and convince you that you can't really be happy unless you buy the sponsors' products.

☐ **Shopping:** A trip to the mall may provide temporary relief but can prove to be a rather costly vacation.

☐ **Sporting Activities (hunting, fishing, golf, tennis, etc.):** These can also be a habit-forming and expensive way to treat anxiety.

☐ **Eating:** Since we have been blessed with such an abundance of food, and such variety, it is little wonder that eating has become America's favorite tranquilizer. The Bible likens using food in this way to drunkenness. "Blessed are you, O land, when your king is the son of nobles, and your princes feast at the proper time—for strength and not for drunkenness!" (Eccl. 10:17).

☐ **Rebound Relationships:** Jumping from one relationship to another as a means of soothing your pain is both selfish (love is about giving, not about getting relief) and foolish. It may actually prolong your misery rather than provide a lasting solution to it.

☐ **Other People:** While Christian fellowship can be a beneficial resource during times of difficulty, care must be taken not to depend more on people than on the Lord.

There are many other things to which we can turn for relief during times of emotional turmoil. But when we look to these pleasures (even the nonsinful ones) more than we look to God to get us through the tough times, we make them idols.

In the Bible, God identifies some of the other "loves" that people have besides Him.[1] Those who are "lovers of pleasure" (2 Tim. 3:4) might look to such things as alcohol, drugs, or sports to get them through a difficult time. Individuals who love money (Luke 16:14; 1 Tim. 6:10; 2 Tim. 3:2) might run to the shopping mall or surf the Internet for bargains. People who love "the praise of men" (John 12:43) may spend time with those who will tell them how wonderful they are or how much they are needed. Those who love food (cf. Prov. 21:17) might raid the refrigerator or run out to the doughnut shop or ice cream parlor for a quick fix. Some people love sleep (Prov. 20:13) and when in distress, they will snooze away their troubles. Those who love the world (1 John 2:15) might look to worldly forms of entertainment such as movies, television, nightclubs, and parties. And let's not forget those whom the Bible refers to as "lovers of themselves" (2 Tim. 3:2), who may turn to forms of self-gratification (especially sexual sin such as fornication, pornography, masturbation, etc.) to ease their pain.

"If all of these are wrong places to find relief, what are the right places?" There is only one right place to turn when you are in distress.

Whom have I in heaven but You?
And there is none upon earth that I desire besides You.
My flesh and my heart fail;
But God is the strength of my heart and my portion forever.
(Ps. 73:25–26)

God alone is the source of your relief. "God is our refuge and strength, a very present help in trouble" (Ps. 46:1). Now, there are a variety of ways in which He may provide that relief, but ultimately He is the One to whom we should turn when seeking refuge in the midst of our trials. We must desire to please Him more than we want relief. The Lord stands willing to help us through our trials. It grieves Him when we turn for help to those weak and worthless objects to which we turned before He saved us.

Here are six ways through which God gives us relief.

God's Word

Reading and studying the Bible and putting into practice what you have learned is the greatest source of help during times of emotional distress. Just listening to Scripture on compact disc or MP3 can provide a good measure of comfort.[2]

Prayer

Praying (if done correctly) focuses our minds on God's attributes, which are a tremendous source of comfort.

Counsel from and Fellowship with Other Christians

One of the most wonderful resources that God has given us is the local church. In addition to biblical preaching and public teaching, the local church provides us with a body of other believers who are capable of providing friendship, accountability, and informal teaching (discipleship and counseling).

Thankfulness

Developing an attitude of gratitude can be an effective tool to counter a host of distressing emotions. Being thankful forces us to think on many of the things listed in Philippians 4:8. A personal *thank* list, containing the many things for which you are thankful, can be a valuable tool. You can carry it with you in your wallet or purse to take out and review regularly.

Biblical Preaching and Teaching

Another resource that God has given us through the church is the ministry of the Word (biblical preaching and teaching). When we sit under biblical teaching, the Holy Spirit uses the spoken Word (as he does the written Word when we read it) to cleanse, convict, sanctify, edify, and encourage us. Good biblical teaching is also available on the radio, on the Internet, on video, and on compact disc and MP3.[3]

Scriptural Tranquilizers

I'd like to introduce you to something that you may never have heard about. Don't worry. It's not a new doctrine—just a new name for an old concept: Scripture memorization. The Bible's tremendous power to calm the anxious heart of a Christian is often minimized. But its power to calm other distressing emotions should not be overlooked.

Any emotion that we are capable of experiencing is identified in Scripture. Specific portions of Scripture can be targeted for virtually every scenario in life. These passages, memorized while in the midst of the emotional distress, can have an even greater tranquilizing effect than if they were read.

Memorizing an appropriate passage of Scripture in the midst of emotional distress enables you to put God's truth into action immediately. When you memorize and meditate on these situation-specific passages, you can draw more flavor out of them. A simple analogy might be comparing memorization and meditation (which, incidentally, involves the concept of a cow chewing its cud) to a piece of Jolly Rancher candy that you can savor for a long time. Bible reading is wonderful, but by comparison, it is a bit more like eating a piece of M&Ms candy. It gives you some quick energy but melts rather quickly in your mouth. When you internalize the Word of God, you give the Spirit of God a more effective weapon with which to fight spiritual battles. "And take . . . the sword of the Spirit, which is the word of God" (Eph. 6:17). The spoken Word is the Spirit's sword—that is, the Word that is on the tip of your tongue because it is in your heart.

The next time you experience distressing emotions, to whom will you turn? The Lord Jesus Christ offers lasting relief, if you will look for it in the right places.

24

Suspicious Mines

Wrath is cruel and anger a torrent, but who is able to stand before jealousy? —Proverbs 27:4

Jealousy is a very powerful and potentially destructive emotion (Prov. 6:32–35; 14:30; Song 8:6) even to the most committed Christian.

There are at least three biblical terms for the word *jealousy*. Two of them (one Hebrew and one Greek) may also be translated as the word *zeal*.[1] All three terms may be correctly rendered as *envy*.

"So what's the difference between zeal, envy, and jealousy?"

To put it simply, *envy* is zeal for that which has been given to another. *Jealousy* is zeal for that which has been given to me. If I am envious, I have a selfish (covetous) zeal for that which belongs to someone else. If I am jealous, I have a zeal for protecting that which I believe is mine (because I am fearful of losing it). Envy and jealousy are like two sides of the same coin.

Heads is envy: the desire to have something that belongs to another (accompanied by varying degrees of resentment). Tails is jealousy: the fear of losing to another that which you already have.

Right or wrong, when a person is jealous, he is afraid of being displaced by someone or something else. When you are jealous of *someone*, it is because you are afraid that the person you love may prefer someone else. When you're jealous of *something*, it is because you are afraid that the thing you're jealous of is going to displace the love (or fondness, or affection, or desire, or whatever) that someone you love has for you. The irony is that if you're jealous, you don't really love that person as much as you think you do because the Bible says, "Love . . . is not jealous" (1 Cor. 13:4 NASB).

Jealousy, like fear, may be righteous or sinful. Remember, God Himself is jealous. "You shall worship no other god, for the LORD, whose name is Jealous, is a jealous God" (Ex. 34:14).

Of course, God is not fearful in a sinful sense, but He is concerned that you and I not displace our love for Him with a love for something else. He knows that if we love anything more than Him, we will be miserable (cf. Eccl. 5:10). His jealousy, therefore, is good, loving, and selfless. It has our best interests in mind.

Another example of righteous jealousy can be seen in the life of the apostle Paul:

> I am jealous for you with a godly jealousy; for I betrothed you to one husband, so that to Christ I might present you as a pure virgin. But I am afraid that, as the serpent deceived Eve by his craftiness, your minds will be led astray from the simplicity and purity of devotion to Christ. (2 Cor. 11:2–3 NASB)

Paul was afraid that his spiritual daughter (the Corinthians), whom he had promised in marriage to Christ, might not remain a virgin until the time of the wedding. He wanted to present his daughter to her Husband as a chaste, pure virgin. His concern was not that of a selfish father who was fearful of losing his dowry, but that of a loving father who was concerned for the spiritual wellbeing of his children, whom he dearly loved.

As a counselor, I am often jealous of my counselees with a godly jealousy. It's not that I'm afraid they will go to someone else who will be able to help them more than I. Rather, I am afraid that the influence of other counselors (professional or otherwise) may lead them away from dependence on the Word of God, and consequently their minds will be led astray from pure devotion to Christ (and His way of solving problems). If I were jealous of other counselors who I knew were counseling them according to the Word of God and could help them as much as if not more than I, that would be sinful jealousy.

The difference between sinful jealousy and godly jealousy has to do with *motive*. You tell me what your motive is and what it is you're afraid of losing, and I'll tell you whether you have the right or wrong kind of jealousy.

Are you afraid of losing something that you deem important?

Are you afraid of losing something that God deems important?

Are you more afraid that those you love will displace you than you are that they will displace the Lord?

Are you more concerned about what you will lose as a result of being displaced than about what the one who displaces you will be losing?

Now, how should you handle potential jealousy over your ex? Probably the first thing to do is to realize that to a greater or lesser degree, you've already been displaced. You cannot allow your heart to be filled with sorrow. Another thing you can do is to pray that your ex will seek his or her primary happiness in the Lord rather than in another person. Perhaps the best thing you can do is to implement the 1 John 4:18 dynamic: "There is no fear in love; but perfect love casts out fear, because fear involves torment. But he who fears has not been made perfect in love."

Since jealousy is a form of fear, its antidote involves loving God and loving your neighbor. You can overcome fear of being displaced by loving God (fulfilling your biblical responsibilities regardless of how you feel) and loving your ex in biblically appropriate ways. Appendix E may provide you with dozens of practical things you can do to overcome jealousy with love.

Examining Envy

Envy is coveting that which belongs to another and being angry with him because he is able to enjoy that which you cannot. Do you remember the parable that Jesus told of the prodigal son(s)? A key point of the story had to do with the sinful attitude of the elder brother. The parable was aimed at the Pharisees, who were complaining that certain tax collectors and other sinners were coming to listen to Jesus. Could it be that they were jealous and envious?

> Now his older son was in the field. And as he came and drew near to the house, he heard music and dancing. So he called one of the servants and asked what these things meant. And he said to him, "Your brother has come, and because he has received him safe and sound, your father has killed the fatted calf." But he was *angry and would not go in*. Therefore his father came out and pleaded with him. So he answered and said to his father, "Lo, these many years I have been serving you; I never transgressed your commandment at any time; and yet you never gave me a young goat, that I might make merry with my friends. But as soon as this son of yours came, who has devoured your livelihood with harlots, you killed the fatted calf for him." (Luke 15:25–30)

Perhaps it was the honor associated with the slaying of the fatted calf, or perhaps it was simply the pleasure associated with the food and merriment of the party, but this elder prodigal son *coveted* something that was given to his brother. The fact that his brother had something he wanted and was not given made him furious.

And so it is with us. Our own covetous desires produce the sins of envy and jealousy (two more of God's built-in smoke alarms to let us know that we may be lusting after something more than we should). The next time you find yourself struggling with these feelings of jealousy toward your ex (or his new "friend"), one of the first questions to ask yourself is: "Have I set my heart on getting him back?"

One of the attending sins[2] of jealousy is *possessiveness*. Jealous people often have a "you belong to me" attitude in their hearts. While there is a certain stewardship of protection that comes with most relationships, stewardship is not the same thing as ownership. It's one thing to protect that which has been entrusted to you by God; it's another to want to possess His property for your own. Will you steal from the Lord that which He has loaned you? Will you use what He has given you to manage for His honor and glory, and the benefit of others, for your own glory, honor, and benefit? Your ex was never yours to do with as you pleased. Remember the words of Job: "Naked I came from my mother's womb, and naked shall I return there. The LORD gave, and the LORD has taken away; blessed be the name of the LORD" (Job 1:21).

25

Isn't That a Shame?

But He gives more grace. Therefore He says: "God resists the proud, but gives grace to the humble." —James 4:6

One of the most unsettling emotions that you may have to deal with right now is embarrassment or shame—especially when in the presence of those who knew you and your ex as a couple. You might have found yourself thinking things like these:

- I don't want to face friends and family members who know we're not together anymore.
- Everybody at the meeting is going to be wondering what I did that caused my ex to dump me.
- If I go there, I'll have to answer all kinds of questions to which I don't know the answers.
- I wonder what my ex told them about the breakup.
- Maybe I should stay away from church for a few weeks to avoid the embarrassment.

A careful study of these thoughts reveals what is often behind embarrassment: selfishness and pride.[1] Embarrassment may be nothing more than a person's heightened self-consciousness over what others will think of him. But often the embarrassment we experience is due to the fact that we're more concerned with our reputation than we should be.[2] Take some admonition from Paul the apostle:

> Let this mind be in you which was also in Christ Jesus, who, being in the form of God, did not consider it robbery to be equal with God, but *made Himself of no reputation*, taking the form of a *bondservant*, and coming in the likeness of men. (Phil. 2:5–7)

While being ashamed or embarrassed is frequently an indication of pride and self-interest, it can also be a good thing. When being embarrassed indicates that we have repented (cf. Rom. 6:21), or leads us to repentance (cf. Ezra 9:6; 2 Thess. 3:14), or motivates us to draw closer to God (cf. Ps. 119:71; James 4:6–7), it becomes our friend. Perhaps the greatest benefit of being embarrassed has to do with the one thing we so despise that we'll do almost anything to avoid being exposed to it: *humiliation*. Being humbled can be a wonderful blessing for the Christian who knows how to respond to it in a godly manner.

Whereas the English words for being ashamed and humiliated connote how a person feels, the Hebrew terms stress more the idea of a person's being *in a state of* humiliation or *in a condition of* being disgraced—especially in a public sort of way.

Of course, the feelings associated with being humiliated are largely the by-product of a person's responses to his circumstances. The degree of embarrassment you feel can be magnified or diminished in degree depending on your interpretation of the humiliating experience and your internal and external responses to it.

Let's consider again the phrase "God resists the proud, but gives grace to the humble." This passage, and others like it (cf. Ps. 138:6; Prov. 3:34; 29:23; Luke 1:52), teaches that God opposes the proud but gives help (supernatural enabling power) to the humble. But this divine assistance is available only to those who know Christ and are willing to walk in humility before Him. It is power to repent of one's former sins, to put off the old man, to be renewed in the spirit of one's mind, to put on the new man, to obey God, to do what the Bible says, to face each day with the assurance that He is causing all things to work together for good, and to be a vibrant witness for Christ and a testimony of His strength even in the midst of trials. This kind of power is available only to those who are willing to *humble themselves* before Him.

I've counted over a dozen occurrences[3] of phrases such as "humble yourselves," "humble ourselves," and "humbled himself" in the Bible. It seems, then, that this notion of humbling ourselves before God is an important one.[4]

> Likewise you younger people, submit yourselves to your elders. Yes, all of you be submissive to one another, and be clothed with humility, for
>
> *"God resists the proud,*
> *But gives grace to the humble."*
>
> Therefore humble yourselves under the mighty hand of God, that He may exalt you in due time, casting all your care upon Him, for He cares for you. (1 Peter 5:5–7)

Here we are commanded to clothe ourselves with humility (much the same way as a servant clothes himself with his apron) and to humble ourselves under God's mighty hand. A time is coming when we will be exalted. Solomon said,

"Before honor is humility" (Prov. 15:33; 18:12). As Jesus put it, "Whoever exalts himself will be humbled, and he who humbles himself will be exalted" (Luke 14:11; see also Luke 18:14; Phil. 2:8). Someday, some way, whether in this life or the next, you will be honored if you respond biblically to this humiliating trial.

Responding biblically to humiliating circumstances usually involves swallowing your pride and humbling yourself in the midst of being humiliated. It means that you rejoice in the opportunity to have God pour out His grace in your life. It means looking forward to potentially embarrassing events to which you must go (and potentially humiliating circumstances that you are unable to avoid) rather than dreading them. Paul said in 2 Corinthians 12:10, "I take pleasure in infirmities, in reproaches, in needs, in persecutions, in distresses, for Christ's sake. For when I am weak, then I am strong." Anticipate the honor that will come in much the same way as Christ, who for the joy that was set before Him endured the cross, despising the shame, made Himself of no reputation, taking the form of a bondservant, and humbled Himself (cf. Heb. 12:2; Phil. 2:7–8).

Is that the way you've been thinking about the embarrassment associated with your breakup? If not, what are you going to tell yourself the next time you begin to feel self-conscious or ashamed about the breakup? Here are a few suggestions:

- I'm not going to make an idol out of my reputation, but am going to commit my reputation to the Lord.
- I'm not going to allow my mind to magnify the embarrassment of this trial to a greater level than it really is.
- Before honor comes humility.
- I'm going to humble myself voluntarily before the Lord humbles me involuntarily.

ISN'T THAT A SHAME?

- I may feel humiliated, but by God's grace I'm going to clothe myself with humility, that He may exalt me in due time.
- I'm not going to resist any opportunities the Lord wants to give me for acquiring more grace; I need all the help I can get.

Let me close this chapter by giving you a few other things you might want to tell yourself when you feel embarrassed by the breakup. In the space provided, see how many biblical responses you can come up with on your own.

- By God's grace, I'm going to get the most mileage out of this humiliating trial. I'm going to consider it a joyous occasion to have my faith tested and be conformed to the image of my Lord Jesus Christ.
- People who truly love me will be more concerned about praying for (and ministering to) me than judging me.
- If God wants me to go to this function (as I believe He does), it would be wrong for me to not go out of selfishness or fear.
- Oh, that my ways were directed to keep Your statutes! Then I would not be ashamed, when I look into all Your commandments. Let my heart be blameless regarding Your statutes, that I may not be ashamed (Ps. 119:5–6, 80).
- I am going to focus all my attention on how I can minister to others rather than on how embarrassed I may feel.
- I should be more concerned about handling this breakup in a God-honoring way (in a way that doesn't embarrass Him) than I am about being embarrassed.

26

Devoted to Who?

Therefore put to death your members which are on the earth: fornication, uncleanness, passion, evil desire, and covetousness, which is idolatry.
—Colossians 3:5

I dolatry is also known as covetousness. In Colossians 3:5, we are told to put to death, among other things, "covetousness, which is idolatry." Paul also makes the two terms synonymous when he says in Ephesians 5:5, "For this you know, that no fornicator, unclean person, nor covetous man, who is an idolater, has any inheritance in the kingdom of Christ and God." What's the connection between the two? A covetous person substitutes his own selfish interests in places that should be occupied by God. He believes that everything and everyone in his life exists for his own benefit.

John Calvin, the Protestant Reformer, referred to the human heart as a factory of idols. God has given us the ability to seek our happiness in anything we choose. We can delight in possessions, activities, ideas, money, pleasure, the approval of others, our work, and even other people. We may delight in Him, His Word, His will, His ways, and His wisdom (cf. Ps. 37:4; 1:2; 40:8; 2 Chron. 17:6; Prov. 8:30). The problem comes when we either seek our happiness in those things that God forbids or seek our happiness in things that God allows more than in Him.

Now, we all know that it's wrong to seek our happiness in things that God expressly forbids—like drunkenness, fornication, or marriage to an unbelieving spouse. But when we delight too much in those things that God allows (like food, money, our jobs, leisure activities and avocations, or even the people we love), we can be guilty of idolatry.

In what do you delight? Personally, I delight in fishing—fly-fishing in particular. Is it a sin to seek a little bit of happiness in this way? Of course not. Everybody knows that fishing is the biblical sport. Some of the apostles were fishermen. (I even heard it said that John, the beloved apostle, was probably a fly fisherman.) Fishing, then, is clearly *not* a sin. But what if, while fishing, I focus on the object of the delight and see God only with my peripheral vision, if at all? Then my focus would be wrong, and I would be in danger of making my fishing an idol. If, on the other hand, I see the object of delight with my peripheral vision, all the while focusing on the gracious God who richly gives me all things to enjoy, and if I use the object as a means to praise my Creator, then I will be worshiping God in my heart rather than an idol.

SELVES   WORK
FOOD   MONEY
PLAY   OTHERS
GOD

If, for example, while floating down the river, I am expressing my gratitude to God for His wonderful creation (the gorgeous countryside, the blue herons swooping across my path, the wood ducks flying overhead, and the beavers and squirrels scampering about), for the time off He has given me from work, for my unselfish wife, who does not complain about the time I spend recharging my emotional batteries by fishing, and for the fish He has allowed me to catch, then my fishing trip becomes a meaningful and genuine worship experience.

What are you coveting to the point of idolatry? Have you made an idol out of anything related to your broken relationship?

- ☐ Your ex?
- ☐ Having a boyfriend or girlfriend?
- ☐ Getting married?
- ☐ Having a truly Christian marriage?
- ☐ Your reputation?
- ☐ Having a godly husband or wife?
- ☐ Not being single or alone?

"Perhaps I do have an idol or two. But how can I tell if I've made an idol out of one of these things—or anything else, for that matter?"

The surest way I know to answer that question is with two other questions.

1. Have you been willing to sin so that you can get what you want?
2. Have you been willing to sin as a result of not being able to get what you want? (Do you become sinfully angry, hateful, vindictive, argumentative, unreasonable, irritable, critical, withdrawn, etc., when you are not able to have what you want?)

If the answer to either of these questions is yes, then you wanted what you wanted *too much*. You chose to do your will rather than God's. You used a privilege or pleasure that God gave you for His glory, and the benefit of others, exclusively for your own glory and/or benefit. Consequently, you are guilty of idolatry. The greater your frequency of sinning (either in an attempt to get what you want or as a result of not being able to get what you want), the greater your sin of idolatry.

"What should I do if I have been guilty of idolatry? How do I dethrone my idol?"

- Ask the Lord to reveal to you any covetous desires (Ps. 139:23).
- Ask yourself the following questions (Lam. 3:40).
  1. What is it that I think I cannot be happy without?
  2. What do I desire, long for, or crave?
  3. What is it that I believe I must have?
  4. What do I spend most of my spare thought time thinking about?
  5. What do I worry most about losing?
  6. In what do I delight (seek my happiness) the most?
  7. What do I love more than I love God and my neighbor?
  8. What am I trusting in more than I'm trusting in God?

9. What do I value the most?
10. What do I hold most dear?
11. To whom do I pay the most honor and respect?
12. To what am I most devoted?
13. On whom am I depending more than I'm depending on God?
14. In what do I seek my refuge (where do I turn for relief)?

• Confess your culpability to God for breaking the first commandments:

And God spoke all these words, saying:
    "I am the LORD your God, who brought you out of the land of Egypt, out of the house of bondage.
    "You shall have no other gods before Me.
    "You shall not make for yourself a carved image—any likeness of anything that is in heaven above, or that is in the earth beneath, or that is in the water under the earth; you shall not bow down to them nor serve them. For I, the LORD your God, am a jealous God, visiting the iniquity of the fathers upon the children to the third and fourth generations of those who hate Me, but showing mercy to thousands, to those who love Me and keep My commandments." (Ex. 20:1–6)

Then one of the scribes came, and having heard them reasoning together, perceiving that He had answered them well, asked Him, "Which is the first commandment of all?" Jesus answered him, "The first of all the commandments is: 'Hear, O Israel, the LORD our God, the LORD is one. And you shall love the LORD your God with all your heart, with all your soul, with all your mind, and with all your strength.' This is the first commandment." (Mark 12:28–30)

• Pray daily that God will help you to dethrone your idols and give you a greater love for Him than for anyone or anything else.

- Remember to view sinful anger and anxiety as divinely installed "smoke detectors" that let you know when you are coveting something to the point of idolatry.
- If your desires conflict with God's desires, choose to give God what He wants rather than giving yourself what you want.
- Learn to replace covetousness with contentment. (The next three chapters will show you how.)

27

Can't Smile Without Who?

I have learned in whatever state I am, to be content:
I know how to be abased, and I know how to abound.
Everywhere and in all things I have learned both to be
full and to be hungry, both to abound and to suffer
need. I can do all things through Christ who
strengthens me.
—Philippians 4:11–13

Some years ago, I developed an inventory so that my counselees would have some idea of the degree to which they were struggling with discontentment. Listed below are twenty-five statements representing various elements of discontentment. After each sentence, place the number that best corresponds to how frequently the statement is true of you.

BIBLICAL CONTENTMENT INVENTORY

RATING SCALE	POINTS
Never (or Hardly Ever)	4
Seldom	3
Sometimes	2
Frequently	1
Always (or Almost Always)	0

1. I am prone to complain when things in my life do not go as I wish. _____

2. I tend to worry when I am faced with the loss of some temporal possession. _____

3. I have difficulty focusing on my God-given responsibilities when things do not go according to my expectations. _____

4. I give in to discouragement rather than trusting God when it seems that my hopes and desires are not going to be fulfilled. _____

5. I am motivated more by how the things I want will please me than how they will glorify God. _____

6. I am willing to sin in order to get what I want. _____

7. I get angry (or have some other sinful attitude) if I do not get what I want. _____

8. I spend most of my spare time every day thinking about material things rather than eternal things. _____

9. I derive more pleasure from thoughts about worldly plenty than I do from my thoughts of Christ, His Word, heaven, and other spiritual things. _____

10. I become more grieved over the loss or lack of material possessions than I do over my sin. _____

11. I talk more about being prosperous in the world than I do about being prosperous in God's eyes. _____

12. I console myself, when in trouble or distress, more with thoughts of worldly provisions than with trust in God and hope of heaven. _____

13. I am more grateful for gifts of temporal significance (money, jewelry, clothing) than for gifts of spiritual significance (biblical counsel, books, instruction). _____

14. I am more concerned with providing for the physical wellbeing of my family than for their spiritual wellbeing. _____

15. I invest a greater portion of my income in worldly pleasures or unnecessary creature comforts than I do in the kingdom of God. _____

16. I become angry in undesirable circumstances that I cannot control. _____

17. I become angry when someone in a position of authority asks me to do something that I don't want to do, and I can't persuade that authority to change his mind. _____

18. I become anxious when I think people are rejecting me, even though I know I've done nothing to offend them. _____

19. I enjoy certain recreational activities so much that I wonder if I could really be happy if I had to live without them. _____

20. I wish others would treat me with more respect than they usually do. _____

21. I wish my life were more interesting or exciting. _____

22. I wish I could enjoy certain sinful activities without feeling guilty. _____

23. I become irritable when people do things that cut into my free time. _____

24. I wish I could live a life of ease with more pleasure than work. _____

25. I think that I have missed God's best for my life or that I will always be trapped in my present circumstances. _____

Total _____

This should give you some idea of how discontent you are. If you scored from 91 to 100, you have no problem with discontentment. (You may have a problem with *dishonesty*!) If you scored from 81 to 90, you are mildly discontent. If your score was from 71 to 80, there are probably some areas of discontentment in your life that need attention. If you scored in the 61–70 range, you may be what the Bible refers to as a covetous man (Eph. 5:5). If your sum is 60 or below, you are in danger of becoming a full-fledged idolater.

"Idolater? That's pretty strong language."

It is indeed. But as I explained in the previous chapter, the New Testament likens covetousness, which is the opposite of contentment, to idolatry.

> For this you know, that no fornicator, unclean person, nor covetous man, *who is an idolater*, has any inheritance in the kingdom of Christ and God. (Eph. 5:5)

> Therefore put to death your members which are on the earth: fornication, uncleanness, passion, evil desire, and covetousness, *which is idolatry*. (Col. 3:5)

It is covetousness (our sinful desire to have more than what God has seen fit to give us) that makes us discontent. Jesus warns in Luke 12:15, "Take heed and beware of covetousness, for one's life does not consist in the abundance of the things he possesses." Jesus is saying that we need to be on guard against our sinful desires to have more than what has been appointed for us to have. Our good, sovereign, loving, and wise heavenly Father knows much better than we do what we need to glorify and enjoy Him now and forever. He knows what will make us happy. He knows how much of a good thing we can handle and how much will tempt us to sin. We don't really know these things, although we often think we do. In his classic book *The Art of Divine Contentment*, Thomas Watson makes some interesting points.

> God sees, in His infinite wisdom, that the same condition is not suitable for all; that which is good for one, may be bad for another; one season of weather will not serve all men's occasions, one needs sunshine, another rain; one condition of life will not fit every man, no more than one suit of apparel will fit every body; prosperity is not fitting for all, neither is adversity. If one man is brought low, perhaps he can bear it better than another can; he has a greater supply of grace, more faith and patience. . . .
>
> Another man is seated in an eminent place of dignity; he is better suited for it; perhaps it is a place that requires a greater measure of judgment, which every one is not capable of; perhaps he can use his estate better, he has a public [open] heart as well as a public place [open home]. The wise God sees that condition to be bad for one, which is good for another; hence it is He who places men in different orbs and spheres; some higher, some lower. One man desires health, God sees sickness is better for him; God will work health out of sickness, by bringing the body of death, into a consumption. Another man desires liberty, God sees restraint better for him; he will work his liberty by restraint; when his feet are bound, his heart shall be most enlarged. Did

we believe this, it would give a check to the sinful disputes and quibbles of our hearts: shall I be discontented at that which is enacted by a decree, and ordered by a providence? Am I going to be a [devoted] child or a rebel?[1]

How discontent are you? What are you coveting? What do you think you need to make you happy? What is it that keeps you from being content right now? Learning how to be content, in whatever state or condition God has placed you, is a must if you are going to learn how to fall out of love biblically. The covetous desires of your heart, if not identified and removed, will seriously impede the healing process. They will give the world, the flesh, and the devil *handles* in your life that can be easily grasped to slow you down as you seek to be free.

In the next two chapters, we will learn what covetousness is and how to replace it with contentment. Before we go there, why not ask God to help you remove those handles of desire that are impeding your ability to fall out of love with your ex and to fall deeper in love with Christ?

28

I Won't Last a Day Without Who?

Now godliness with contentment is great gain. For we brought nothing into this world, and it is certain we can carry nothing out. And having food and clothing, with these we shall be content. —1 Timothy 6:6–8

What does it mean to be content?

Think in terms of a pizza pie that has been cut into seven slices. Each slice differs slightly in size and content, but they must be baked together for the pie to be prepared correctly. So it is with the seven definitions of contentment that we'll be sampling together.

Now, you may not have realized it, but you've already sampled the first two slices of the pie in previous chapters. So let me briefly mention them before we go on to the other five.

Definition number one (from chapter 8): Contentment is realizing that true satisfaction can come only from

building my life around those things that cannot be taken away or destroyed.

> Do not lay up for yourselves treasures on earth, where moth and rust destroy and where thieves break in and steal; but lay up for yourselves treasures in heaven, where neither moth nor rust destroys and where thieves do not break in and steal. For where your treasure is, there your heart will be also. (Matt. 6:19–21)

Security and contentment are related to building one's life around things that endure for eternity rather than things that last for the moment. The more you build your life around temporal things, the more insecure and discontent you will be.

Definition number two (from chapter 26): Contentment is delighting in God more than in anything else.

"Delight yourself also in the Lord, and He shall give you the desires of your heart" (Ps. 37:4). God gives us the ability to delight ourselves (seek our happiness) in virtually anything—a person, a vocation, a hobby or recreational activity, an automobile, a home, travel, or anything else on which we set our heart. It is wrong to delight in these things if you seek your happiness more in them than you do in the Lord. If the object of your delight is something other than the Lord, then you are likely making an idol out of your pleasure. If you focus your delight on the object itself, that is where your worship will end. But if you can see your object of delight while focusing on God Himself, who richly gives you all things to enjoy, and if you use the object as a means to praise your Creator, then you will be worshiping God rather than your idol.

Definition number three: Contentment is realizing that God has already provided everything I need to glorify and enjoy Him.

Think about it. God has already given you everything you need to be truly happy. The minimum requirements for your contentment, according to 1 Timothy 6:8, are food and clothing. Do you not have much more than these? If you are a Christian, you have the Holy Spirit to comfort and assist you. You have the Word of God to teach, convict, correct, and instruct you in righteousness. You have brothers and sisters in your local church to encourage you along life's difficult journey. You have the promises of God to give you hope. And you have the assurance of spending all eternity with Christ in heavenly bliss. You may not have appropriated all His provisions yet, but if you are a believer, He has provided you with "all things that pertain to life and godliness, through the knowledge of Him who called us by glory and virtue" (2 Peter 1:3).

"But I still don't have everything I want to be truly happy! I want a special companion with whom I can share my life."

Remember, our definition says that God has provided you with everything you need, not with everything you want. People in our day routinely confuse the two. Many things we believe to be needs are not identified as such in the Bible. In fact, you would probably be more biblically accurate if you were to substitute the word *desire* for the word *need* as it appears in most modern Christian literature. Jesus told Martha, "You are worried and troubled about many things. But one thing is needed"—to sit at the feet of Christ and hear His words (Luke 10:41–42).

So what are you waiting for to be happy? "I would be happy if only _____." God will provide, in His time, whatever is necessary for your long-term happiness. "And my God shall supply all your need according to His riches in glory by Christ Jesus" (Phil. 4:19).

Definition number four: Contentment is being able to adjust the level of my desire to the condition and purpose chosen for me by God.

> I am not saying this because I am in need, for I have learned to be content whatever the circumstances. I know what it is to be in need, and I know what it is to have plenty. I have

learned the secret of being content in any and every situation, whether well fed or hungry, whether living in plenty or in want. (Phil. 4:11–12 NIV)

Paul learned an important element of contentment: the ability to regulate his level of desire to the circumstances into which God chose to place him from day to day. One day he might be living in plenty; the next he might be living in want of something he had the day before.

Thomas Watson again is very helpful as he teaches us to regulate our fancy.

> It is the fancy which raises the price of things above their real worth. What is the reason one tulip is worth five pounds, another perhaps not worth one shilling? Fancy raises the price. The difference is rather imaginary than real. So, why should it be better to have thousands than hundreds, is because men fancy it so. If we could fancy a lower condition better, as having less care in it, and less accountability, it would be far more desirable. The water that springs out of the rock drinks as sweet as if it came out of a golden chalice. Things are as we fancy them.
>
> Ever since the fall, the fancy is distempered. God saw that the imagination of the thoughts of his heart were evil. Fancy looks through the wrong spectacles. Pray that God will sanctify your fancy. A lower condition would make us content if the mind and fancy were set correctly.[1]

So what is the condition into which God has recently led you? What is God's purpose for your life right now? To what fancy are you having a difficult time adjusting?

I know that you desire those "lovin' feelings" for your ex to go away. I'm sure you want the pain to diminish. There may be a dozen other things you desire at this moment that were yours before the breakup. But right now, you can begin to prayerfully adjust the level of those desires according to God's purpose for your life and the circumstances into which He has placed you. Don't allow them to interfere with the divine program. Perhaps tomorrow your condition will be different. Perhaps tomorrow God will reveal other purposes for your life and ministry. Tomorrow, He may give you the desires of your heart. But for today, work hard to turn down the thermostat on the temporal and turn up the register on the eternal.

29

I Don't Need to Be in Love

Let your conduct be without covetousness; be content with such things as you have. For He Himself has said, "I will never leave you nor forsake you." —Hebrews 13:5

I am indebted to Jeremiah Burroughs, the great Puritan author, who in his classic, *The Rare Jewel of Christian Contentment*, provides us with the last three slices of the pie.

Definition number five: Contentment is willingly submitting to and delighting in God's wise and loving disposal in every condition of life.

> Then Job arose, tore his robe, and shaved his head; and he fell to the ground and worshiped. And he said:
>
> "Naked I came from my mother's womb,
> And naked shall I return there.

185

The LORD gave, and the LORD has taken away;
Blessed be the name of the LORD."

In all this Job did not sin nor charge God with wrong. (Job 1:20–22)

Job didn't blame his calamity on any of the immediate causes (the Sabeans, or the fire that fell from heaven, or the Chaldeans, or the great wind that came from across the wilderness, or the devil himself). Rather, he saw God as the One who controlled all circumstances.

Burroughs develops this theme:

The one who has learned this lesson of contentment looks *up* to God in all things. He does not *look down* at the instruments and means, so as to say that such a *man* did it, or that it was the unreasonableness of such and such *instruments*, or it was similar cruel treatment by so and so. But he *looks up* to God. A contented heart looks to God's disposal. That is, he sees the wisdom of God in everything. In his submission to God, he sees His sovereignty, but what enables him to take pleasure [in the trial] is God's wisdom. The Lord knows how to order things better than I. The Lord sees further ahead than I do. I see only the present but the Lord sees a great while from now. And how do I know but that had it not been for this affliction, I should have been undone. I know that the love of God may as well stand with an afflicted condition as with a prosperous condition. There are reasonings of this kind in a contented spirit, submitting to the disposal of God.[1]

Your broken relationship didn't take God by surprise. In fact, God, in His infinite wisdom and love, was providentially at work in the circumstances of your breakup. The sooner you submit to His sovereign will[2] in this matter, the sooner you will be able to overcome discontentment and much of the misery associated with it.

Definition number six: Contentment is knowing how to use the things of the world without being engrossed in them.

> But this I say, brethren, the time is short, so that from now on even those who have wives should be as though they had none, those who weep as though they did not weep, those who rejoice as though they did not rejoice, those who buy as though they did not possess, and those who use this world as not misusing it. For the form of this world is passing away. (1 Cor. 7:29–31)

Paul is addressing some questions the Corinthians had about marriage. In light of the "present distress" (the coming[3] persecution of the church by the Emperor Nero), he urges unmarried individuals to remain single if at all possible. Part of his argument has to do with not getting too attached to the comforts of this world. Once again, Jeremiah Burroughs hits the bullseye.

Do not be inordinately taken up with the comforts of this world when you have them. When you have them, do not take too much satisfaction in them. There is a certain principle: However inordinate any man or woman is in sorrow when a comfort has been taken from them, so were they inordinate in their rejoicing in the comfort when they had it. For instance, God takes away a child and you are inordinately sorrowful, beyond what God allows in a natural or Christian way. Now although I never knew before how your heart was towards the child, yet when I see this, though you are a stranger to me, I may without breach of charity conclude that your heart was immoderately set upon your child or husband, or upon any other comfort that I see you grieving [inordinately] for when God has taken it away. If you hear bad news about your estates, and your hearts are dejected immoderately, and you have a discontented mood because of such and such a trial, certainly your hearts were immoderately set upon the world. So, likewise, for your reputation, if you hear others report this or that evil about you, and your hearts are dejected because you think you suffer in your name, your hearts were inordinately set upon your name and reputation. Now therefore, the way for you to not be immoderate in your sorrow when afflictions come is to not be immoderate in your love and delights when you have prosperity.[4]

So how is it with you? Have you allowed yourself to be pre-occupied with the comforts of this life? Do you view the things that God has given you to enjoy as a means to an end (to glorify God) or as an end in themselves?

Definition number seven: Contentment involves putting the best possible interpretation on God's dealings with you.

In 1 Corinthians 13, we read that love "believes all things." That means that you believe the best about others. In other words, if there are ten possible interpretations or explanations as to why someone took a particular course of action, nine of them being evil and only one of them being good, the loving person will, in the absence of real evidence to the contrary, choose to reject the bad and believe the good. Now, if we are commanded to view other sinners with this kind of optimism, how much more should we put the best possible interpretation on God's dealings with us? How much more should we forsake the bad interpretations of His providence in our lives and accept the good ones?

Let's take a look at what Burroughs has to say about contentment.

If any good interpretation can be made of God's ways toward you, make it. You think it serious if you have a friend who always makes bad interpretations of your ways towards him. You would take that rather hard. . . . It is a very tedious thing to the Spirit of God when we make such bad interpretations of His ways toward us. When God deals with us otherwise than we would have Him do, if one sense [that is] worse than another can be put on it, we will be sure to do it. Thus, when an

I DON'T NEED TO BE IN LOVE

affliction befalls you, many good senses may be made of God's works towards you. You should think this way: "It may be God intends only to test me by this," or "It may be God saw that my heart was too set on something, and He intends to show me what is in my heart," or "Perhaps God saw that if my wealth continued I would fall into sin (that the better my position was, the worse my soul would be)" or "It may be God intended only to bless me with some special grace" or "It might be that God intends to prepare me for some great work which He has for me." This is how you should reason.

But we, on the contrary, make bad interpretations of God's dealings with us, and say, "God doesn't mean [to bless me like] this. Surely the Lord intends to display His wrath and displeasure against me by this trial. This is just the beginning of further evil He has determined against me!" Just as they said in the wilderness [you say to the Lord]: "You have brought us here to slay us." This is the worst interpretation you can possibly make on God's ways. Oh, why will you make these the worst interpretations, when there may be better? . . .

I urge you to consider that God does not deal with you as you deal with Him. If God were to put the worst interpretation on all your ways towards Him as you put on His towards you, it would be very bad for you.[5]

Learning to be content isn't easy. But in the final analysis, it is easier than being discontent. You will spare yourself a great deal of misery and will find it much easier to recover from the breakup as you become increasingly more content with your present circumstances.

"That would be great. But is there anything else I need to know about being content?"

You've probably got enough to contemplate for now, but in the final two chapters, we will address another character trait that is closely related to contentment.

30

You Can't Hurry
Out of Love

For you have need of endurance, so that after you have done the will of God, you may receive the promise.
—*Hebrews 10:36*

"I've tried it God's way, and it doesn't work!" I hear this a lot from my counselees.

"Really? What exactly did you do?"

"Oh, I did ABCDEFG."

"I see. But I thought you did it God's way."

"I did!"

"Well, what else did you do?"

"I told you I did ABCDEFG!"

"But what about HIJKLMNOP?"

"HIJKLMNOP? Does God expect me to do that, too?"

"The Bible says you should. May I show you where?"

People are often surprised to learn that what they've done to solve their problems is not a complete scriptural solution. Solving problems God's way usually involves not only putting off sinful behaviors but also putting on biblical alternatives.

Now, every once in a while, the conversation in my office goes something like this:

"I've tried it God's way, and it doesn't work!"

"Really? What exactly did you do?"

"Oh, I did ABCDEFGHIJKLMNOP."

"Now, wait a minute. You did ABCDEFGHIJKLMNOP and it didn't work?"

"That's right."

"And how long did you do it?"

"Oh, I'd say for about a week and a half."

"That's not long enough to solve a habitual problem like yours. You have need of endurance so that *after* you've done the will of God—not while you're doing it for a week and a half, but after you've done it day in and day out for a longer period of time—you may receive the promise."

Endurance is something that we don't hear much about today—except perhaps in the arena of athletics. But the Bible has a lot to say about it (and its little cousin, patience). These two character traits are almost always found in the context of trials. We can usually see the need for patience in our lives when we go through big trials, but we don't always make the connection between our need for patience and the little trials of life (such as when another motorist cuts us off in traffic, or when someone keeps us waiting for ten or fifteen minutes).

"Is there a difference between endurance and patience?"

Although they are used interchangeably in some New Testament English translations, the primary Greek word for *endurance* is a military term that has to do with bearing up under suffering, while the principal word for *patience* carries with it the idea of being steadfast and long-suffering. Another interesting distinction that some make between the two is that *endurance* is used for being patient in circumstances, whereas *patience* refers to patience with people.[1] According to 1 Corinthians 13, if you love God, not only will you be patient with Him, you will also "endure all things" that He decides to put you through.

As we did with contentment, let's describe patience from several different perspectives.

Patience is the ability to rejoice in the knowledge that your present distress will produce godly character that is of great value not only in this life, but also in the next.

Do you see any relationship between the trial that you are currently going through and your ultimate happiness?

> My brethren, count it all joy when you fall into various trials, knowing that the testing of your faith produces patience. But let patience have its perfect work, that you may be perfect and complete, lacking nothing. (James 1:2–4)

Trials pressure us to develop patience. Patience allows us to endure the trials all the way through to the end, at which time we become complete or mature. The more mature we are (the more we respond to life's trials as Christ would), the happier we'll be.

> We also glory in tribulations, knowing that tribulation produces perseverance; and perseverance, character; and character, hope. (Rom. 5:3–4)

What's more, your character will have great value, not only in this life, but also in the next.

For bodily exercise profits a little, but godliness is profitable for all things, having promise of the life that now is and of that which is to come. (1 Tim. 4:8)

Most of us don't spend enough time thinking about heaven. And yet the New Testament abounds with passages relating this life to the next. Over and over again, we read verses that admonish us to live godly lives during our short time on earth in light of an eternity in heaven.

So the next time you're tempted to murmur or complain about the depth of your trial, think about heaven. When you get there, you'll probably wish you'd had a few more trials down here to pick up additional crowns.

Patience is the ability, while experiencing physical pain or mental turmoil, to keep your emotions (grief, fear, and anger) from developing into sinful thoughts, words, attitudes, or actions (especially toward God).

When we are ill, it becomes easier to sin and harder to obey God. Job responded admirably after he lost his children and his possessions. But once Satan was allowed to afflict his body with boils (chapter 2), he started to justify himself rather than (or before) God. Job ultimately endured the trial and repented of his sinful attitude.

Elijah was courageous while God was using him to humiliate the prophets of Baal in 1 Kings 19. But the next chapter finds him sitting under a broom tree, depressed, afraid, and suicidal. What happened? He was no doubt physically exhausted as a result of all the work involved in preparing the altar upon which God sent down fire. (Check it out for yourself.) Then he went on a ninety-mile run for his life to Beersheba. When the angel of the Lord came to him in the desert, he didn't chide Elijah for having a sinful attitude, but simply instructed him to eat and sleep.

Of course, we should never use our illnesses or weaknesses as an excuse to sin because God has promised to give us all the grace we need to obey Him in every kind of trial we might face.

Patience is the ability to keep a biblical perspective about your troubles by not magnifying a tolerable trial so that it appears to your mind as an intolerable one.

The word *true* in Philippians 4:8 ("whatever is true ... think about such things" [NIV]) has as one of its meanings "that which conforms to reality." It is the opposite of perceiving as reality the unrealistic fantasies that your mind is capable of imagining. One of the secrets to endurance is taking care not to feel a pinprick in your finger as though you had been stabbed in the arm. A number of people in the Bible looked at their trials through magnifying glasses.

- Cain said to the Lord, "My punishment is greater than I can bear!" (Gen. 4:13).
- When Rachel saw that she bore Jacob no children, she envied her sister and said to Jacob, "Give me children, or else I die!" (Gen. 30:1).
- Moses said to the Lord, "Why have You afflicted Your servant? And why have I not found favor in Your sight, that You have laid the burden of all these people on me?" (Num. 11:11).
- Elijah said, "I have been very zealous for the LORD God of hosts; for the children of Israel have forsaken Your covenant, torn down Your altars, and killed Your prophets with the sword. I alone am left; and they seek to take my life" (1 Kings 19:10).
- It displeased Jonah that the Ninevites repented, and he became angry. So he prayed to the Lord, "Ah, LORD, was not this what I said when I was still in my country?

Therefore I fled previously to Tarshish; for I know that You are a gracious and merciful God, slow to anger and abundant in lovingkindness, One who relents from doing harm. Therefore now, O LORD, please take my life from me, for it is better for me to die than to live!" (Jonah 4:2–3).

Some breakups, especially of a marriage, are among the most difficult trials that a person can endure. But if you are a Christian, your trial is not intolerable. As we will see in the next and final chapter, God will not allow you to be tempted to that degree.

31

Someday Your Prince
Will Come

But as it is written: "Eye has not seen, nor ear heard, nor have entered into the heart of man the things which God has prepared for those who love Him." —1 Corinthians 2:9

In the previous chapter, I made the point that if you love God, you will be patient with Him. In this chapter, I'm going to drive that point home as hard as I can. You're probably acquainted with the familiar passage of Scripture above. You may even know that it is a quotation from the book of Isaiah. But did you know that the Holy Spirit has altered the verse as He, through the apostle Paul, penned a significant modification of the original?

"What do you mean, He altered it?"

I mean that He changed the language. He replaced one word with another word. See if you can figure out what I'm talking about. Here is the original quotation from Isaiah 64:4. "For since the beginning of the world men have not heard nor perceived by the ear, nor has the eye seen any God besides You, who acts for the one who waits for Him."

Do you see it? Look at the last line. The phrase *waits for Him* was changed to *love Him*. The person that Isaiah says waits for God is the same person that Paul says loves God. If you love God, you will wait for Him. If you are impatient with God, you don't love Him as you should. According to 1 Corinthians 13, the first element of love is patience. Below are two more definitions of patience.

Patience is the ability to endure tribulation without resorting to any sinful means of deliverance.

An angry and suspicious King Saul was wrongly pursuing David in 1 Samuel 24. Notice how David responded to this trial.

> Now it happened, when Saul had returned from following the Philistines, that it was told him, saying, "Take note! David is in the Wilderness of En Gedi." Then Saul took three thousand chosen men from all Israel, and went to seek David and his men on the Rocks of the Wild Goats. So he came to the sheepfolds by the road, where there was a cave; and Saul went in to attend to his needs. (David and his men were staying in the recesses of the cave.) Then the men of David said to him, "This is the day of which the LORD said to you, 'Behold, I will deliver your enemy into your hand, that you may do to him as it seems good to you.'" And David arose and secretly cut off a corner of Saul's robe. Now it happened afterward that David's heart troubled him because he had cut Saul's robe. And he said to his men, "The LORD forbid that I should do this thing to my master, the LORD's anointed, to stretch out my hand against him, seeing he is the anointed of the LORD." So David restrained his servants with these words, and did not allow them to rise against Saul. And Saul got up from the cave and went on his way. (1 Sam. 24:1–6)

David didn't use any sinful means to deliver himself from Saul's unjust persecution—even though others urged him to do so. Rather than letting himself out of the cave by murdering his predecessor, he patiently waited for the Lord to extricate him in His time. David really loved the Lord. God said of him, "I have found David the son of Jesse, a man after My own heart, who will do all My will" (Acts 13:22, quoting Ps. 89:20; 1 Sam. 13:14).

What sinful means of deliverance from your trial have you been tempted to employ?

- Lying your way back into the relationship
- Compromising your convictions
- Manipulating your ex
- Promising to do anything to get your ex back
- Gossiping about (or slandering) your ex
- Threatening to do yourself harm
- Selfishly jumping into a rebound relationship
- _____
- _____

Don't be like King Saul, who took matters into his own hands. Be like David, who loved the Lord and waited for Him to do what He promised.

Patience is the ability to accept a difficult situation from the Lord without accusing Him of wrongdoing or giving Him a deadline to remove it.

The first chapter of the book of Job finds Job losing his children and his possessions, then bowing down in worship before the Lord. The last verse reads, "In all this Job did not sin nor charge God with wrong."

Do you complain when things don't go your way? Have you been guilty of murmuring against the Lord because of the breakup?

Trials can be like boxes into which the Lord places those He loves. In *The Complete Husband*, I wrote about how to respond when going through such a trial.

You are in a box. You're cramped, uncomfortable, and becoming increasingly more frustrated with each passing hour. You want the pressure you're feeling to be lifted so you can have some relief. You want God to get you out of the box for good! The Bible has some very important things to say to you about that box.

> "No temptation has overtaken you but such as is common to man; and God is faithful, who will not allow you to be tempted beyond what you are able, but with the temptation will provide the way of escape also, that you may be able to endure it" (1 Cor. 10:13).

The first thing God wants you to know is that you're not the only one who has ever been encased in the kind of box you are in. The trouble you're in isn't new. It is "common to man." That is, although it may have a few unique components, it is, nonetheless, a kind of trouble (box) that has imprisoned many others before you. Indeed, even as you read this, there are others (yes, even other Christians) who are basically in the same box as you are right now.

Another thing God tells you in this verse about your box is that He has limited the trouble you are in, and He has done that in two very important ways. This divine promise, however, applies to you only if you are a Christian—that is, if you are, by faith, depending only on the redemptive work of Christ on the cross for your salvation.[1] If so, then He has limited your trouble in *scope*, and He has limited it in *duration*.

LIMITED IN SCOPE

LIMITED IN DURATION

God's faithfulness to you means first of all that He "will not allow you to be tempted beyond what you are able." That is, He will not allow the temptation to become so difficult that you will not be *able* to deal with it biblically (in a way that is not sinful and will bring glory to God). In other words, He will not let your box become so small that it will crush or smother you!

Secondly, God's faithful promise to you is that as a Christian, your trial will come to an end. He will "provide the way of escape . . . that you may be able to endure it." God promises that someday, some way, your trial will end. He says that someday He is going to let you out of the box.[2] He doesn't tell you *how* He's going to do it. He doesn't tell you *when*—only that He *will* do it.

Sooner or later, God is going to let you out of the box. He may provide your way of escape by sending a bulldozer crashing through the wall. He may push a button, which will silently trigger a trapdoor in the floor of the box. He may send a giant can opener to tear off the top of the box and throw a ladder down for you to climb out. Perhaps He will send an army of angels to march around the perimeter of your box and, after a shout, the walls will come crashing down like the walls of Jericho. He may simply snap His fingers, and the entire box will disappear.

While you're waiting for God to get you out, are you cooperating with His plan or, like so many, have you impatiently pulled out your pocketknife in an attempt to tunnel your way out of the box before God, through righteous means, extricates you in His own way?[3]

Yes, my friend, someday our prince will come. The Lord will return and will reward us for our faithfulness to Him. Someday, perhaps before He returns, He will let you out of the box in which you are currently trapped—as long as you cooperate with His purposes for your life. It is my prayer that the Holy Spirit will use the biblical resources in this book to help you patiently prepare for that day. May you learn how to fall out of love with the wrong things and grow more and more in love with the Savior!

Appendix A

What Am I Doing the Rest of Your Life?

T his appendix is for those of you who are dealing with the heartaches associated with divorce. There are issues unique to the breakdown of a marriage that must be given special attention. I will attempt to briefly address a few of those issues here.

First let me make an important distinction between two kinds of individuals: those whose marriages are *in the process* of coming to an end and those whose marriages have already *ended* in divorce. Please keep in mind that this book was written to help people get over the hurts associated with the termination of a relationship. It therefore applies principally to those whose marriages have already ended in divorce. In cases in which a divorce has not yet been finalized, the believer has a much wider scope of responsibilities to consider than those delineated in this book. Issues such as what can be done to save the marriage, whether or not church discipline is an option, to what extent one should seek pastoral,[1] marital, and legal counsel, what part one may take in the participation of a divorce (a marriage is a very difficult thing to terminate without sinning), and how to minister to the children during this difficult time of transition must be more predominant concerns than dealing with the personal pain associated with the loss of a marriage partner.

The breakup of a marriage involves the severing of a one-flesh relationship. There is no other human relationship as intimate as marriage. To be one flesh with someone is to be one person with him. You and your spouse experienced a level of companionship that exceeded every other human relationship in life. The two of you shared a bed, a home, food, money, dreams, goals, desires, feelings, fears, struggles, and even your bodies. Now all of that has changed. You find yourself alone, without the intimate companionship of another person. You have no one with whom to share things at that deep level to which you had grown accustomed. You have lost not just a close friend, but a part of yourself. The Bible offers hope and help for the intense loneliness and sorrow that often accompanies divorce.

You may have to contemplate more seriously than others (whose relationship did not involve marriage vows or children) the possibility of reconciliation with your ex.[2] While you may want to get over your ex, you may have to leave open the possibility of remarriage. Admittedly, this is a difficult task. You will find it more difficult to follow some of the instructions in this book than if reconciliation were not a viable option. Pay special attention to what I have written about not becoming bitter toward your ex and about loving him/her more now than before (chapters 5, 13, 14, and 15). While you should plan for the future based on the facts as they are, do not set those plans in concrete. A change of heart on the part of your ex may alter those plans significantly (cf. James 4:13–17).

If you have children, your ex is probably going to be a part of your life for a long time. This continual contact will trigger all manner of temptation to sin in thought, word, and deed, and may even lengthen the time it will take to displace the sorrow in your heart. Routine contact with your ex will be especially difficult if you do not have a clear conscience and have not sincerely forgiven your ex for all that he/she has done to hurt you. Even if you have fulfilled all your biblical responsibilities, your ex may try to make life miserable for you. By God's grace, endure these hostilities, using all His available resources to overcome evil with good (Rom. 12:21).

Divorce can be the most difficult of all relationship losses to deal with—especially for the person who didn't really want the union to end. It can be even more difficult than the death of a spouse. The grief that a person experiences as the result of death is not typically as protracted as in the case of divorce. Before death, the hurt, rejection, guilt, and bitterness experienced by the widow-to-be is not near the level that usually exists for the person going through an unwanted divorce. But perhaps the greatest reason that divorce is so difficult to handle has to do with the fact that divorce is typically not as abrupt and final as is death. At least for a while, the divorced spouse dies in the heart every day. There may be times when reconciliation seems promising. This engenders additional hope, which may be appropriate, but can cause disappointment (cf. Prov. 13:12) if no remarriage occurs.

There are other issues unique to divorce, which you may have to face. Guilt over having failed in marriage, uncharitable judgments from well-meaning Christians who view divorce as an almost unpardonable sin, and unloving attitudes from self-righteous individuals who may treat you as a second-class citizen in the kingdom of heaven are problems not addressed specifically in this book but whose solutions will be covered in principle.

Recuperating from divorce will require total dependence on God's grace. But if you are a Christian, you have at your disposal His unlimited resources. You have the mind of Christ (1 Cor. 2:16), and He will get you through this trial.

Appendix B

It's Not Too Late to Turn Back Now

Perhaps you are trying to gain control over romantic feelings for someone with whom you've cheated on your spouse? If so, there is hope for your situation. Many unfaithful spouses I've helped over the past several decades wondered two things:

- Can I ever get over these powerful feelings I have toward the other woman/man?
- Will I ever be able to love my spouse with the same kind of intensity I have for the other person?

If you are a Christian who is truly willing to do what the Bible says, the answer to both of these questions is *yes*.

When you met and married your spouse, you, in effect, opened up a lifetime savings account at a brand-new bank: First National _____ (insert the name of your spouse in the blank). You soon began to make some rather large investments in her/his account. You invested a good deal of time, effort, thought, money, and even your own body. You also placed in the safety deposit box of that bank many of your valuables along with the . majority of your secret treasures. And for a while, perhaps a good long while, you were pleased with the interest you received on your investments.

Then, little by little, after becoming disillusioned with the returns you were receiving on your principal, you slowed down the frequency with which you deposited your assets. Perhaps you even stopped making new investments and simply tried to live off the interest for a while.

Then one day, you received information quite unexpectedly about a brand-new bank that had just opened a branch close to where you work (or golf, or play tennis): First Federal _____ (insert the name of the other person to whom you gave your heart and/or body in the blank). This new bank promised to give you a much better return on your investments—especially in those areas where the other bank had disappointed you.

You began investigating all the additional perks that First Federal had to offer. The list seemed quite impressive. So before you knew what you were doing (and before you counted the costs), you opened up a First Federal account—you signed on the dotted line without carefully reading the fine print. Little by little, you began making additional deposits in this new bank. It wasn't long before you were taking your assets out of First National and moving them to First Federal. First National, on more than one occasion, brought to your attention the indisputable fact that your principal investment with it was dwindling considerably. Of course, you denied it and tried to shift the blame back to First National. But deep down in your heart, you knew who was really at fault.

For a while, it helped to remind yourself that First National wasn't quite as good a deal as you thought it would be when you opened up your first account with it. You had convinced yourself long ago that First National would probably never be able to provide you with the returns that you were looking for.

But be that as it may, now you're in a real quandary. It's as Jesus said it would be: "Where your treasure is, there your heart will be also" (Matt. 6:21). You now have investments in both banks, and consequently your heart is torn between the two of them—you have feelings for both persons.

So what are you going to do? If you want God's best (and if you want the answers to those two questions I raised at the beginning of this appendix to be *yes*), you will have to take two very important steps.

1. Totally close the account at First Federal.
2. Systematically redeposit every last investment that was made in First Federal back into First National.

You must completely end the adulterous affair. This other person must be told plainly that the relationship is over. If possible, ask for forgiveness (preferably on a conference call with your spouse or pastor on the line) for your selfishness and deceit. There can be no continuing communication (no secret rendezvous, telephone calls, cards, letters, or e-mails). The other person should be emphatically told not to contact you anymore. You must be willing to amputate from your life anything that will tempt you to reopen this illegal bank account.

Jesus, after explaining to the disciples that lusting for a woman was adultery of the heart, said this to His disciples:

> If your right eye makes you stumble, tear it out and throw it from you; for it is better for you to lose one of the parts of your body, than for your whole body to be thrown into hell. If your right hand makes you stumble, cut it off and throw it from you; for it is better for you to lose one of the

parts of your body, than for your whole body to go into hell. (Matt. 5:29–30 NASB)

He told them that they must remove anything from their lives that made them stumble into sin—even if it's something they cherished (cf. Eph. 5:29). Don't keep any mementos, photographs, keepsakes, or other memorabilia that might tempt you to spend time thinking about (and fueling romantic feelings for) the other person. You may have to change your telephone number, your e-mail address, or the route you take to and from the office. I've known several men and women who were even willing to give up their jobs in order to take this important step.

Having closed the illegal account, you must next begin the process of systematically transferring all your assets back to the original bank. Exactly how much of your money, time, thoughts, dreams, affection, initiative, and creative energies did you invest in the other person's account? They will all have to be reinvested with your spouse. Did you buy the other person gifts? Ask yourself, "What kind of gifts can I buy for my spouse?" Did you go on dates with the other person? Ask yourself, "Where can I take my spouse out for a date?" Did you call the other person from/at work? Ask, "When are the best times for me to surprise my spouse with a telephone call?" How many hours did you spend thinking about what you could do to please the other person? Spend that much time thinking about what you can do to adore and please your spouse. And perhaps most importantly, how much time did you spend revealing your heart to the other person and listening intently as she revealed her heart to you? Invest the same amount of time in the revelation process with your spouse. Are you willing to invest the effort and creativity necessary to make these kinds of redeposits? If you're serious about obeying God, you will be willing to invest whatever it takes to repair your marriage. Like Zacchaeus (Luke 19:8–10), your willingness to make restitution will be an indication of the sincerity of your repentance.

If you want your feelings to change, you must begin to court your spouse as vigorously as you courted the other person. After they've changed, continue courting him "as long as you both shall live."

"OK, I see what you are saying, but when I think of all those promises I made to the other person—for the most part with every intention of keeping them—I feel so guilty."

The fact that you feel guilty is probably a *good* thing. It means that you've not yet totally defiled your conscience. Not unlike a computer virus, your sin may have simply misprogrammed your conscience to believe that you owe the other person more than you really do. But you are more indebted to your spouse than you are to the other adulterer. You owe God even more than that. You may have made promises[1] to the other person for which you must ask forgiveness for breaking. But breaking your vow to God and lifetime covenant with your spouse will have further-reaching consequences than breaking a rash promise to your adulterous lover (cf. Eccl. 5:1–7).

"But I can't just abandon her. That wouldn't be Christian!"

Closing the bank account is not abandonment. Your pastor or another biblical counselor is in a much better position to minister to the other person than you are. If you truly are concerned about the welfare of the other individual, turn him over to the care of a pastor or other biblical counselor. You are not qualified to help in this situation. The other person has also sinned, and may be in need of repentance. Don't stand in the way of God's divine discipline by trying to remove the culpability and consequences of his sin (cf. Heb. 12:1–11).

> Do not be deceived, God is not mocked; for whatever a man sows, that he will also reap. For he who sows to his flesh will of the flesh reap corruption, but he who sows to the Spirit

will of the Spirit reap everlasting life. And let us not grow weary while doing good, for in due season we shall reap if we do not lose heart. Therefore, as we have opportunity, let us do good to all, especially to those who are of the household of faith. (Gal. 6:7–10)

If you are willing to take these two steps, then you will benefit from reading this book. If you are not willing, as much as is possible, to close First Federal and reinvest in First National, it is doubtful that you will ever fully "fall out of love" with your former lover. May God grant you the humility, courage, and grace to make the right choice.

Appendix C

You'll Never Get to Heaven If . . .

The next few pages contain information that could impact your life more profoundly than anything else you have learned in this book. Please read them carefully.

Many people believe that getting to heaven is accomplished by doing good things and relatively few bad things. The truth is, however, that even one sin is enough to keep you out of heaven. It really doesn't matter how much good you do; any sin—regardless of how great or small—is enough to keep you out of heaven and send you straight to hell.

> Through one man sin entered into the world, and death through sin, and so death spread to all men, because all sinned. (Rom. 5:12 NASB)

> For the wages of sin is death, but the free gift of God is eternal life in Christ Jesus our Lord. (Rom. 6:23 NASB)

> For whoever keeps the whole law and yet stumbles in one point, he has become guilty of all. For He who said, "Do not commit

adultery," also said, "Do not commit murder." Now if you do not commit adultery, but do commit murder, you have become a transgressor of the law. (James 2:10–11 NASB)

According to the Bible, for a person to be saved and go to heaven, there must first be the realization that his sin has caused a separation from God. God, who is both holy and just, must deal with sinners and their sin appropriately. God's holiness disposes Him to hate sin. His justice requires Him to punish sin. The wages or punishment of sin is death (cf. Gen. 2:17; Rom. 5:12; 6:23). For Him to simply overlook sin without requiring the proper punishment would go against His holy and just nature.

How just would you consider a judge to be if he, out of partiality to a convicted serial murderer, sentenced him to only a few days in jail rather than sentencing him (at least) to the minimum sentence required by the law?

Well, what kind of magistrate would God, "the Judge of all the earth" (Gen. 18:25), be if He didn't punish sinners who transgress His law? For God to let sinners off the hook without demanding that they pay at least the minimum penalty for their crimes would render Him unjust (and unfit for the bench). Since the minimum sentence for sin, according to the Bible, is death, God must punish sinners. His justice requires Him to do so.

It is appointed for men to die once and after this comes judgment. (Heb. 9:27 NASB)

The Lord knows how to rescue the godly from temptation, and to keep the unrighteous under punishment for the day of judgment. (2 Peter 2:9 NASB)

Then I saw a great white throne and Him who sat upon it, from whose presence earth and heaven fled away, and no place was found for them. And I saw the dead, the great and the small, standing before the throne, and books were opened; and another book was opened, which is the book of life; and the dead were judged from the things which were written in the books, according to their deeds. And the sea gave up the dead which were in it, and death and Hades gave up the dead which were in them; and they were judged, every one of them according to their deeds. Then death and Hades were thrown into the lake of fire. This is the second death, the lake of fire. (Rev. 20:11–14 NASB)

Now, there are other elements of God's nature that dispose Him to be loving and merciful. In fact, the Bible says that God is "not willing that any should perish but that all should come to repentance" (2 Peter 3:9).

"But how can He forgive sinners in love and mercy when His justice requires Him to punish them for their sins?"

God had to find a substitute—someone who was willing to pay the penalty in the place of sinners.

Men of Israel, listen to these words: Jesus the Nazarene, a man attested to you by God with miracles and wonders and signs which God performed through Him in your midst, just as you yourselves know—this Man, delivered over by the predetermined plan and foreknowledge of God, you nailed to a cross by the hands of godless men and put Him to death. But God raised Him up again, putting an end to the agony of death, since it was impossible for Him to be held in its power. (Acts 2:22–24 NASB)

If God could find someone willing to pay the price for men's sin, yet who did not have to die for his own sin, He could punish that substitute in the sinner's place. But who is without sin? Only God. So God, in His love and mercy, took upon Himself the form of a man in the person of Jesus Christ (Phil. 2:7). The Lord Jesus lived a sinless life and then sacrificed Himself on the cross as the substitute for sinners who were incapable of redeeming themselves. After He was buried, He rose from the dead and in so doing demonstrated His power over death and sin and hell. "For Christ also died for sins once for all, the just for the unjust, so that He might bring us to God, having been put to death in the flesh, but made alive in the spirit" (1 Peter 3:18 NASB).

This resurrection power is available to those who truly are willing to let go of their sins and believe the gospel (the good news about what Christ did by dying on the cross). The gospel of Jesus Christ provides power not only over death and hell, but also over sin—the very sin that has enslaved people and caused them so much misery.

Have you ever turned away from your sin and asked God to forgive you once and for all on the basis of Christ's substitutionary death on the cross?

> For God so loved the world, that He gave His only begotten Son, that whoever believes in Him shall not perish, but have eternal life. . . . He who believes in the Son has eternal life; but he who does not obey the Son will not see life, but the wrath of God abides on him. (John 3:16, 36 NASB)

> If you confess with your mouth Jesus as Lord, and believe in your heart that God raised Him from the dead, you will be saved; for with the heart a person believes, resulting in righteousness, and with the mouth he confesses, resulting in salvation. . . . For "Whoever will call on the name of the Lord will be saved." (Rom. 10:9–10, 13 NASB)

When a person becomes a Christian, the Holy Spirit indwells (takes up residency inside of) him, giving him the power to obey God. Your ability to make use of the biblical resources contained in this book will be severely limited if you do not have the Spirit's enabling power in your life. He is the true Comforter. He can come alongside you and assist you in your efforts not only to fall out of love with your ex, but also to live the kind of life that is pleasing to Him.

> Therefore, having been justified by faith, we have peace with God through our Lord Jesus Christ, through whom also we have obtained our introduction by faith into this grace in which we stand; and we exult in hope of the glory of God. And not only this, but we also exult in our tribulations, knowing that tribulation brings about perseverance; and perseverance, proven character; and proven character, hope; and hope does not disappoint, because the love of God has been poured out within our hearts through the Holy Spirit who was given to us.
>
> For while we were still helpless, at the right time Christ died for the ungodly. For one will hardly die for a righteous man; though perhaps for the good man someone would dare even to die. But God demonstrates His own love toward us, in that while we were yet sinners, Christ died for us. (Rom. 5:1–8 NASB)

Appendix D

You Always Hurt the One You Don't Love[1]

The following checklist will help you identify some of the ways you might have sinned against your ex. Although not exhaustive, it represents some of the common areas of sinful behavior and neglect among people involved in interpersonal relationships. The wording is in the first person to facilitate confessing your sins directly to the offended party at the appropriate time. As you prayerfully read over each item, put a check next to those offenses that you believe are applicable to you. Fill in any blank spaces with more precise information. Confess each transgression to God and then prepare your heart to confess them, when appropriate, to your ex.

The more specific you can be, the more likely it is that your ex will realize the degree to which you are serious about changing and the extent to which you are cognizant of how your sins have hurt him. The more specifically you can identify your bad habits, the easier it will be for you, by God's grace, to change.

Add to the list any additional offenses that are not mentioned specifically. When you are finished, look back over the checked items for specific patterns of behavior that may indicate a dominating sin such as selfishness, anger, irresponsibility, or lack of self-control.

General Failure List for Relationships

- ☐ I was not a good example of a Christian.
- ☐ I've been bitter and unforgiving toward you.
- ☐ I didn't often admit when I was wrong.
- ☐ I failed to realize why _____ is so important to you.
- ☐ I didn't ask for your advice or opinion as often as I should have.
- ☐ I didn't show enough concern for your interest in _____.
- ☐ I've been hypocritical with you in regard to _____.
- ☐ I became irritable with you about _____.
- ☐ I was lazy in _____.
- ☐ I had unreasonable expectations, such as _____.
- ☐ I didn't express myself clearly and thoroughly.
- ☐ I often interrupted you when you were talking.
- ☐ My attention often wandered when you were talking to me.
- ☐ I was often too preoccupied with _____.
- ☐ I was too harsh with you.
- ☐ I was impatient with you, especially when _____.
- ☐ I raised my voice rather than responding to you softly and graciously.
- ☐ I used biting sarcasm when I spoke to you.
- ☐ I responded to you before I understood what you were really saying. I rebuked you publicly rather than trying to lovingly correct you in private.

- ☐ I judged your thoughts and motives without knowing them.
- ☐ I didn't cover in love (or overlook) many of the things you did that irritated me. I didn't put the best possible interpretation on the things you did but tended to be critical and even suspicious of you at times.
- ☐ I lectured and criticized you when you did something wrong rather than lovingly comforting you and encouraging you to change.
- ☐ I used manipulation and intimidation to win arguments rather than trying to resolve conflicts biblically.
- ☐ I said and did things that were vindictive in nature, such as _____.
- ☐ I teased you too much in front of others.
- ☐ I murmured and complained about _____.
- ☐ I was too critical of your family.
- ☐ I didn't make enough effort to get along with your family.
- ☐ I was selfish when it came to offering you help but often expected you to help me whenever I needed it.
- ☐ I wasn't very sensitive to your problems, moods, and feelings.
- ☐ I seldom expressed my appreciation for you or complimented you.
- ☐ I said unkind things to you.
- ☐ I said unkind things about you.
- ☐ I was not totally truthful with you about _____.
- ☐ I called you names.
- ☐ I was too legalistic, especially in the area of _____.
- ☐ I made excuses or simply refused when you asked me to do certain things that you wanted me to do, such as _____.
- ☐ I had bad manners, especially when it came to _____.

- ☐ I criticized you for your faults and mistakes rather than investing the time and effort to lovingly help you correct them.
- ☐ I got angry or withdrew or _____ when a problem or disagreement arose between us.
- ☐ I blamed you for my mistakes, such as _____.
- ☐ I was too distrustful of you, especially when it came to _____.
- ☐ I was too sensitive because of my pride.
- ☐ I took things too seriously and often made mountains out of molehills, such as _____.
- ☐ I didn't try to overcome your evil (sin) with good.
- ☐ I didn't make ministering to you enough of a priority.
- ☐ I led you into sexual sin.

Additional Failure List Items for Former Husbands

- ☐ I didn't lead our family in devotions regularly.
- ☐ I had a closer relationship (I was more "one flesh") with _____ in some ways than I had (was) with you.
- ☐ I didn't give you enough assistance with _____.
- ☐ I neglected your desire/need for _____.
- ☐ I didn't show you my love in the tangible ways that I know please you, such as _____.
- ☐ I didn't give you enough assistance with _____.
- ☐ I took your love for granted by _____.
- ☐ I didn't nourish you or cherish you as the Bible commands me to do.
- ☐ I was too dependent on my parents for _____.
- ☐ I was lazy in doing _____.
- ☐ I was selfish sexually.
- ☐ I expected you too often to drop what you were doing and give me attention.

☐ I became irritated when you were not ready to leave on time, but expected you to be patient when I was not ready on time.

☐ I didn't give you enough candy, flowers, gifts, and surprises.

☐ I didn't keep my _____ neat and orderly.

☐ I didn't treat you as though you were a fragile vessel.

☐ I didn't show you enough respect, especially by _____.

☐ I didn't show you enough affection in our home.

☐ I didn't show you enough affection in public.

☐ I didn't make it a point to spend time every day having significant communication with you.

☐ I spent too much time away from home.

☐ I was slow to offer you help with the housework and dishes.

☐ I made important decisions without your counsel.

☐ I teased you too much in front of others.

☐ I left food, clothing, and other items lying around the house.

☐ I played music too loudly.

☐ I didn't exercise leadership in our family in that I _____.

☐ I invested too much time trying to advance my career.

☐ I didn't take you out to dinner or shopping or _____ often enough.

☐ I was too critical of your family.

☐ I didn't make enough effort to get along with your family.

☐ I didn't invest enough time in trying to advance my career.

☐ I was selfish when it came to offering you help but often expected you to help me whenever I needed it.

☐ I gave in to depression rather than trying to overcome it.

☐ I wasn't very sensitive to your problems, moods, and feelings.

☐ I wasn't as sympathetic as I should have been to your _____.

☐ I seldom expressed my appreciation for you or complimented you.

☐ I spent too much money on _____.

☐ I was too stingy with my money in that I _____.

☐ I didn't try hard enough to find things for us to do together.

☐ I showed too much interest in other women by _____.

☐ I used profanity.

☐ I drank too much.

☐ I smoked too much.

☐ I watched too much television.

☐ I made excuses or simply refused when you asked me to do certain things that you wanted me to do, such as _____.

☐ I had bad manners, especially when it came to _____.

☐ I was difficult to satisfy when it came to _____.

☐ I got angry or withdrew or _____ when a problem or disagreement arose between us.

☐ I was too ambitious about _____.

☐ I blamed you for my mistakes, such as _____.

☐ I didn't seek help when I had a serious problem.

☐ I became angry when you didn't discipline the children as I thought you should.

☐ I didn't invest enough time discussing with you our philosophy of raising children.

☐ I didn't cultivate the children's friendship enough.

☐ I was inconsistent when it came to disciplining the children.

☐ I didn't teach or discuss God's Word with the children as often as I should have.

☐ I didn't spend enough time playing with the children.

☐ I didn't help you enough with the children's _____.

☐ I did not follow through with promises I made to you and the children.

☐ I didn't give enough of my _____ to the church.

☐ I didn't invest enough time cultivating biblical friendships for us to enjoy.

☐ I lost my temper or _____ when you or the children did not treat me with respect.

☐ I wasn't "easily entreated" (easy to be appealed to) by you or the children.

☐ I was often unreasonable with you or the children.

☐ I didn't do enough reading that would have helped me improve as a husband, father, and Christian.

☐ I compared you and the children unfavorably with others.

☐ I didn't work hard enough at correcting my annoying habits and mannerisms, especially _____.

☐ I didn't take care of myself physically as I should have.

☐ I didn't express my love to you when I didn't feel love for you.

☐ I didn't protect you enough, especially in the area of _____.

☐ I didn't always remember birthdays, anniversaries, and other special occasions.

☐ I sometimes resisted or resented your helpful suggestions.

☐ I didn't handle our family finances biblically, especially in the area of _____.

☐ I didn't run errands gladly.

☐ I allowed my anxiety over your safety and the safety of the children to selfishly prohibit you from doing certain things, such as _____.

225

Additional Failure List Items for Former Wives

- ☐ I didn't read my Bible as often as I should have. My personal devotions and quiet time were not a priority in my life.
- ☐ I didn't attend church services with a joyful spirit. I allowed the confusion of getting the family ready to interfere with my attitude.
- ☐ I resented the fact that we lived where we did. (I didn't trust God, that in His sovereignty, He had placed us where He wanted us to be.)
- ☐ I was angry and bitter about _____.
- ☐ I demanded too much from you in the area of _____.
- ☐ I didn't praise you enough for _____.
- ☐ I concealed how I really felt about _____.
- ☐ I resented being tied down by the children.
- ☐ I resented that we didn't have children.
- ☐ I was too bossy with you or the children about _____.
- ☐ I didn't reveal my heart to you in the area of _____.
- ☐ I was too concerned about outward appearances and how others viewed us.
- ☐ I was too concerned about money and dealt with it inappropriately by _____.
- ☐ I spent too much time on _____.
- ☐ I spent too much money on _____.
- ☐ I used gestures and facial expressions that clearly showed disrespect.
- ☐ When I was not feeling 100 percent, I avoided doing those things that you wanted or needed me to do for you.
- ☐ I was too moody.
- ☐ I was apt to use my hormonal changes as an excuse to sin against you.
- ☐ I was a perfectionist about my housekeeping.

- ☐ I was a poor housekeeper and didn't take proper care in the appearance of our home.
- ☐ I wasn't your best friend.
- ☐ I was more intimate (one flesh) in some ways with _____ than I was with you.
- ☐ I was unwilling to go _____ with you, or to do _____ when you wanted.
- ☐ I was abrupt in my speech rather than being gentle.
- ☐ I was not patient with you—especially about those things I would have most liked to see you change.
- ☐ I was too contentious about _____.
- ☐ I never really accepted or liked your family.
- ☐ I was sarcastic in my responses when I didn't agree with you.
- ☐ I was more concerned with pleasing my parents than I was about pleasing you.
- ☐ My job was more important to me than our marriage.
- ☐ _____ was more important to me than being a wife and mother.
- ☐ Your job was of little interest to me, so I resented discussing it with you when you came home from work.
- ☐ I argued with you about _____ rather than being respectful and submissive.
- ☐ I contradicted you in public.
- ☐ I didn't always pay attention when you were telling me things that didn't interest me.
- ☐ I failed to understand why _____ is so important to you.
- ☐ I didn't attempt to share your interest in _____.
- ☐ I didn't give you assistance with _____.
- ☐ I neglected your need/desire for _____.
- ☐ Pleasing God was not the first priority in my life.
- ☐ I used my "womanly wiles" to get my own way.

- ☐ I was too dependent on my parents for _____.
- ☐ I didn't accept your role as the leader of our home.
- ☐ Even if I knew it would hurt you, I went to great lengths to get my own way.
- ☐ I made decisions without first asking you for guidance.
- ☐ I made decisions without considering God's will.
- ☐ I took your love for granted.
- ☐ I was lazy when it came to _____.
- ☐ I sometimes forgot to do things that you asked me to do.
- ☐ I was irritable with you about _____.
- ☐ I was quick to judge your motives.
- ☐ I was selfish sexually.
- ☐ I expected you to always be on time.
- ☐ When we were going somewhere and I was running late, I resented it if you said anything to me.
- ☐ I became irritated when you didn't always stop what you were doing if I wanted to discuss something with you.
- ☐ When you were discouraged, I was unwilling to be an encouragement to you.
- ☐ I was unreasonable about _____.
- ☐ I put the children's needs ahead of yours.
- ☐ I failed to consider you when I decorated our home.
- ☐ I complained that we weren't able to eat out the way we did before the children were born.
- ☐ I made important decisions without your counsel.
- ☐ I manipulated you to get what I wanted.
- ☐ I didn't express affection the way you wanted me to.
- ☐ I didn't enthusiastically support your role as leader of our home.
- ☐ I was contentious about the way you spent money.
- ☐ I criticized you in front of the children (and/or our friends).
- ☐ I didn't put forth enough effort to get along with your family.

- ☐ I called your siblings names or referred to them in ways that are not biblical.
- ☐ I was more concerned about the children's physical and social wellbeing than I was about their spiritual wellbeing.
- ☐ I didn't give the children the attention they needed.
- ☐ I didn't arrange to spend time alone with you when you came home from work.
- ☐ I didn't demonstrate to the children that my relationship with you was the primary relationship in our home.
- ☐ I didn't discipline our children in accordance with biblical principles and/or your desires.
- ☐ I was inconsistent in the discipline of our children.
- ☐ I knew that _____ annoyed you, but was too stubborn and/or selfish to change.
- ☐ I argued with you in front of the children.
- ☐ I worried too much about the things the Lord has promised He will provide.
- ☐ I expected you to "grovel" before I would consider forgiving you.
- ☐ I physically abused you when I didn't get my own way.
- ☐ I was inconsiderate of your desires.
- ☐ I allowed negative issues to overshadow the positive.
- ☐ I was far too serious about _____.
- ☐ I stopped listening to you when I didn't like what you wanted to discuss.
- ☐ I blamed you for things that were my fault.
- ☐ I lost my temper frequently.
- ☐ I often made unreasonable demands on you and expected too much.
- ☐ I often refused to have sexual relations and rarely initiated them.
- ☐ I refused to go _____ with you.
- ☐ I made promises to the children that I didn't keep.

☐ I made promises to you that I didn't keep.

☐ I expected you to know what I needed and wanted.

☐ I expected you to know my thoughts, opinions, feelings, and concerns without expressing them to you.

☐ I sometimes flirted with other men to make you jealous or to make myself feel good about my desirability to other men.

☐ I complained about your lack of _____.

☐ I used profanity.

☐ I took the Lord's name in vain.

☐ I smoked too much.

☐ I drank too much.

☐ I often didn't admit when I was wrong.

☐ I was legalistic—especially in the area of _____.

☐ I watched too much (or inappropriate) television.

☐ I allowed the children to watch too much (or inappropriate) television.

☐ I was not easily satisfied.

☐ I seldom expressed appreciation to you and didn't compliment you as I should have.

☐ I had bad manners when it came to _____.

☐ I was not totally truthful with you about _____.

☐ I didn't discuss the Bible with the children enough.

☐ I didn't spend enough time playing with the children.

☐ I compared you unfavorably to others.

☐ I didn't work hard enough at correcting my annoying habits and mannerisms.

☐ I often neglected your sexual needs, and was interested only in my own.

☐ I got my feelings hurt very easily (I was sensitive because of my pride).

☐ I didn't handle money in a responsible way.

☐ I complained about running errands for you.

- ☐ I was selfish about wanting all your free time.
- ☐ I didn't take proper care of myself physically.
- ☐ I refused to ask your advice about _____.
- ☐ I became resentful when you tried to hold me accountable.
- ☐ I became sinfully angry when _____.
- ☐ I expected you to help me with the children even when I knew you were tired.
- ☐ I was pessimistic in my outlook about _____.
- ☐ I complained about our church.
- ☐ I argued with you even when I knew you were right.
- ☐ I didn't confront your sin.
- ☐ I didn't have a meek and quiet spirit.
- ☐ I compared myself and our life with others.
- ☐ Even though I knew diet and exercise would benefit me greatly, I didn't consistently practice self-control in these areas.
- ☐ I gave in to depression or _____ rather than trying to fight it (I listened to the lies I told myself rather than talking to myself biblically).
- ☐ I was discontent.
- ☐ I read books and magazines that promoted worldly and humanistic values.
- ☐ I was jealous of the godly way that _____ treated _____ and was resentful and angry that you didn't treat me the same way.

Appendix E

You Don't Have to *Say* "I Love You"

⌒⌒

In 1 Corinthians 13, we find a description of what love *does*. From the biblical perspective, love is more a verb than a noun. Fifteen descriptive verbs about love are found in verses 4–7 of this famous "love chapter."[1] Eight of the fifteen are stated negatively (love is/does *not* . . .); seven are stated positively (love is/does . . .). The negative descriptions imply their positive counterparts as the positive descriptions imply their negative counterparts (lack of love). In other words, being patient with someone means that you will not be impatient, and "not seeking its own" implies that love will seek the interests of the person who is being loved. Since you, for the most part, will be loving your ex in absentia, you will usually find yourself loving him more through the negative means than through the positive ones.

Listed below are eighty-eight specific things that you may still be able to do (or not do) for your ex as an expression of biblical love. They are categorized under the fifteen elements of love found in 1 Corinthians 13:4–7. Depending on your exact set of circumstances, some of these suggestions will be unfeasible, impractical, or impossible to accomplish. In certain cases, and with certain individuals, it may even be unwise (if not dangerous) to attempt them. But perhaps there are a few items on the list that you've not yet considered for your unique situation. There is also space for you to add some of your own applications for each facet of love.

Love is patient

- ☐ I will not lose my temper (have a short fuse) when my ex doesn't _____.
- ☐ I will be forbearing with my ex's foibles and idiosyncratic behaviors.
- ☐ I will restrain my angry words and actions when my ex does something selfish.
- ☐ I will not write off my ex if he/she doesn't immediately see things from my point of view.
- ☐ I will continue to pray for my ex's bad attitudes until the Lord changes them (or until He changes my ability to handle them biblically).
- ☐ _____.
- ☐ _____.

Love is kind

- ☐ I will not be overcome by evil but will overcome my ex's evil with good. (I will not retaliate in a sinful way.)
- ☐ I will say kind things about my ex.
- ☐ I will offer to run errands for my ex.
- ☐ I will express sympathy and concern to my ex when he/she is in the midst of trouble (rather than gloating that he/she is finally getting what he/she deserves).

☐ I will be considerate of how my future decisions will affect my ex. (I will not ignore my ex's interests or feelings.)

☐ I will not be excessively passive toward my ex but will actively look for God-honoring ways to be a blessing to him/her.

☐ I will not be cruel or malicious to my ex.

☐ _____.

☐ _____.

Love does not envy

☐ I will not become resentful if God sees fit to bless my ex with the things for which I am longing.

☐ I will rejoice in God's goodness toward my ex, remembering that it was the goodness of God that led me to repentance (cf. Rom. 2:4).

☐ I will offer to share something I have with my ex.

☐ I will pray that my ex will succeed in a particular area of his/her interest.

☐ I will not allow myself to focus on what I have lost as a result of the breakup, but will rather imagine how the Lord may use the breakup for good in both of our lives.

☐ I will pray that both of us will learn how to seek our happiness in the Lord.

☐ I will remind myself that my ex was never one of my possessions but was temporarily loaned to me by the Lord.

☐ _____.

☐ _____.

Love does not brag

☐ I will not go out of my way to let my ex know that "I'm doing just fine" without him/her.

☐ I will not inordinately seek my ex's approval.

- ☐ I will not make my ex's approval the barometer of my happiness or success.
- ☐ I will not put my ex down in order to make myself look good.
- ☐ I will keep quiet about the achievements that God has wrought in my life since the breakup.
- ☐ I will acknowledge to others my own sinful contributions to the breakdown of our relationship.
- ☐ I will not play the martyr.
- ☐ If I boast about anything, it will be of how God is using the breakup in my life to make me more like Christ.
- ☐ _____.
- ☐ _____.

Love is not arrogant

- ☐ I will ask my ex for advice from time to time.
- ☐ When my ex reproves or criticizes me, I will not get defensive but will acknowledge my faults and if necessary ask for his/her forgiveness.
- ☐ I will give glory to God for anything for which my ex commends me.
- ☐ I will not make unfair or unrealistic demands from my ex.
- ☐ I will not make my ex grovel for my forgiveness. ("Look, Buddy/Betsey, you haven't offended any ole body, you offended *me* . . . and my anger is not easily propitiated!")
- ☐ I will be grateful for any kindness that my ex may show me.
- ☐ I will pray that my ex will grow to love the Lord more than I pray that he/she will grow to love me.
- ☐ I will guard my heart against having a critical, censorious, condemning attitude toward my ex.
- ☐ _____.
- ☐ _____.

Love does not act unbecomingly

- ☐ I will make every effort to be courteous to my ex whenever I am in his/her presence.
- ☐ I will not say or do anything to disgrace or embarrass my ex.
- ☐ I will be a good Christian model for my ex.
- ☐ I will not gossip about or slander my ex to others.
- ☐ I will not resort to sarcastic, profane, condescending, or disrespectful forms of communication, but will seek to build up (edify) my ex whenever appropriate.
- ☐ _____.
- ☐ _____.

Love does not seek its own

- ☐ I will not manipulate my ex.
- ☐ I will not beg my ex to come back.
- ☐ I will not try to make my ex jealous.
- ☐ Whenever I have opportunities to show love to my ex, I will examine my motives to be sure that I'm not giving in order to get something back.
- ☐ I will not waste time dwelling on how my ex doesn't love me or appreciate me.
- ☐ I will not allow fear of what my ex might take from me to prevent me from seeing (and perhaps meeting) his needs.
- ☐ I will not superimpose my will for my ex over God's will for him/her.
- ☐ _____.
- ☐ _____.

Love is not provoked

- ☐ I will not talk to my ex when I'm upset with him/her but will wait until my anger is under control.

- ☐ I will remind myself from time to time about my ex's good qualities.
- ☐ I will think before I speak to my ex when he/she does or says something to push my buttons.
- ☐ I will make sure that I am well rested, "prayed-up," not in an irritable mood, and not sinfully angry at anyone before I converse with my ex.
- ☐ _____.
- ☐ _____.

Love does not take into account a wrong suffered

- ☐ I will forgive my ex (either verbally or in my heart) for every hurtful thing that he/she has done to me.
- ☐ I will not bear a grudge against my ex.
- ☐ I will not review in my mind the hurtful things that my ex did to me during our relationship.
- ☐ I will not try to console myself by talking to others about my ex's faults.
- ☐ _____.
- ☐ _____.

Love does not rejoice in unrighteousness

- ☐ I will not take pleasure in any foolish decisions that I learn my ex has made.
- ☐ I will not take pleasure in any hurtful things that others do to my ex.
- ☐ I will not take pleasure in any injustice that befalls my ex.
- ☐ I will not take pleasure in any acts of vengeance against my ex that my sinful heart may imagine.
- ☐ I will not take pleasure in any thought of others' sinning against my ex.
- ☐ _____.
- ☐ _____.

Love rejoices in the truth

- ☐ I will not be unfair when dealing with my ex but will treat him/her with justice and equity.
- ☐ I will not unfairly side with others against my ex but will defend him/her against any false accusations.
- ☐ I will stand up for the truth when contending with my ex about issues that violate my convictions.
- ☐ I will be more loyal to the truth than to my ex or to any person involved in the breakup.
- ☐ I will not allow my mind to fantasize about things involving my ex that either are sinful or do not conform to reality.
- ☐ _____.
- ☐ _____.

Love bears all things[2]

- ☐ I will not view this breakup as something intolerable, unbearable, or beyond my ability to handle as a Christian.
- ☐ I will not take personally every offense that my ex commits against me.
- ☐ I will make every effort to patiently put up with my ex's sins, foibles, and idiosyncrasies.
- ☐ I will make every effort to cover my ex's sins, foibles, and idiosyncrasies with love.
- ☐ _____.
- ☐ _____.

Love believes all things

- ☐ I will not be unduly suspicious of my ex.
- ☐ I will make it a point to put the best spin on my ex's behavior unless I have hard evidence to the contrary.
- ☐ I will not jump to hasty and unfounded conclusions about my ex.

☐ I will not judge my ex's motives.
☐ I will not criticize my ex if he/she does something that the Bible does not say is sinful.
☐ Believing that God can transform the worst of sinners, I will reject the mind-set that says, "I will *never* make myself vulnerable to my ex again as long as we both shall live."
☐ _____.
☐ _____.

Love hopes all things

☐ I will pray regularly for my ex.
☐ I will not waste time trying to figure out all that is wrong in (or what can go wrong in) my ex's life.
☐ I will look for ways that God may be working through the breakup for His glory.
☐ I will look for ways that God may be working for the good of my ex.
☐ I will look for opportunities to give biblical hope to my ex.
☐ I will choose to believe that God is working all things together for the good of those who love Him and are called according to His purpose and that someday (in this life or the next) I will see exactly how He has done so.
☐ _____.
☐ _____.

Love endures all things

☐ I will not allow this breakup to keep me from fulfilling my biblical responsibilities toward my ex.
☐ I will not allow my hurt feelings to cloud my ability to interpret (and respond to) life's circumstances from God's point of view.

☐ I will commit myself to maintaining Christlike attitudes toward my ex.

☐ I will not allow the wrong my ex has done to cause me to conclude that he/she is beyond God's ability to save or restore.

☐ I will remind myself often that suffering is a part of the Christian life and thank God that He has seen fit to use my ex to "examine" my life, that I might realize where I need to become more like the Lord Jesus Christ.

☐ _____.

☐ _____.

Additional Expressions of Love

☐ _____.

☐ _____.

☐ _____.

☐ _____.

☐ _____.

☐ _____.

Notes

Introduction: Your Achin', Breakin' Heart

1. Continually reminding yourself of your ex's faults violates 1 Corinthians 13:5—love "does not take into account a wrong suffered" (NASB)—and increases the likelihood that you will become bitter.

Chapter One: How Can I Mend My Broken Heart?

1. The chapter titles in this book are spoofs of some popular song titles and are not intended to be an endorsement of the unbiblical lyrics they may contain.

2. I've thought long and hard about whether or not to use the word *ex* in this book. Apart from its not being a biblical term, the word (which is slang for *former spouse or partner*) disturbs me a bit because of its association with such concepts as *exclude, exile, expel, expire, expunge, exterminate,* and *expendable*—all of which have connotations that might not fall in line with the biblical way to think about another person. However, because of its accepted usage in modern nomenclature and since I've not been able to identify an exact English synonym that expresses the idea so succinctly, I've decided to use it, with one proviso. As you come across this term in your reading, I'd like to ask you to think of it as an abbreviation for the word *examiner*. That is, I'd like you to view your ex as the person whom the Lord has chosen to examine you. According to the dictionary, the word *examine* means "to determine the qualifications, aptitude, or skills of by means of questions or exercises." From now on, why not try to think of your former sweetheart as the person whom the Lord has used (and is using) to

test your character for the purpose of revealing to you your strengths and weaknesses (cf. Job 31:6; Ps. 139:23; Prov. 17:3; 1 Peter 1:7).

Chapter Two: Have You Tossed Those Lovin' Feelings?

1. For additional aspects of self-control (slices of the self-control pie), obtain a copy of the author's audio recording "A Biblical View of Self-Control," available from Sound Word Associates, (219) 548-0933, http://www.soundword.com/index.html.

Chapter Three: How Do Fools "Fall in Love"?

1. Falling in love is not a biblical construct. People don't "fall in love" in the sense that a person might accidentally fall into an open manhole. Moreover, what many people today call "falling in love" might more accurately be called "falling into lust." The Bible does, however, make reference to the intense and passionate romantic/erotic kind of love that can exist between a man and a woman (cf. Song 3:1–4; 8:1–7).

2. Lou Priolo, *The Complete Husband* (Amityville, NY: Calvary Press, 1999), 85–87.

Chapter Four: Only *Love* Can Break a Heart?

1. The emotions themselves are technically not "negative" but natural. We perceive them as negative because of their distressing nature.

2. In his Gospel, Mark uses at least four different Greek words to describe the Lord's anger.

Chapter Five: Can't I Stop Loving You?

1. Implicit in each of the negative elements of love is its antithetical positive counterpart.

2. The Greek word for *patience* has to do with being "long-tempered." We might say that a patient person has a long fuse instead of a short one. The patient person exercises self-control by restraining his angry passions, especially in stressful situations.

3. For an excellent treatment of all fourteen characteristics of 1 Corinthians 13 love in a brief package, see Jay Adams, *Update on Chris-*

tian Counseling, vol. 2 (Phillipsburg, NJ: Presbyterian and Reformed, 1981), 35–48.

Chapter Six: Love Isn't Blue

1. Guilt is not primarily a feeling. It is first and foremost man's culpability before a holy God. Guilt makes people feel nervous, unhappy, and miserable.

2. Forgiveness deals directly with man's guilt. Sanctification deals with man's corruption and thereby helps to eliminate guilt that is associated with being in bondage to sin. As we see our lives being brought into conformity to Jesus Christ, any guilt associated with particular enslaving sins we know we will likely commit in the future is purged from our consciences.

3. When a person is born again and places his faith in Christ, all his sins (past, present, and future) are forgiven. He no longer relates to God primarily as a criminal relates to a judge. Instead, he is placed in a relationship with God whereby he relates to Him as a son does to his father. When he sins as a Christian, the fatherly relationship is affected. Confession must therefore be made and forgiveness sought so that the fatherly relationship may be restored. "*Our Father* in heaven, . . . forgive us our debts, as we forgive our debtors. . . . For if you forgive men their trespasses, your *heavenly Father* will also forgive you. But if you do not forgive men their trespasses, neither will *your Father* forgive your trespasses" (Matt. 6:9, 12, 14, 15).

4. She and her husband have graciously granted me permission to include their story in this book.

5. God's decreed will sometimes involves allowing others to sin against us. "Him, being delivered by the determined purpose and foreknowledge of God, you have taken by lawless hands, have crucified, and put to death" (Acts 2:23).

6. For more information, see my audio series, *How to Improve Your Looks from the Inside Out*, available from Sound Word Associates, (219) 548-0933, http://www.soundword.com.

Chapter Seven: Why Are You Lonesome Tonight?

1. Of course, our communication with God *does* go both ways. We speak to God in prayer. He speaks to us through the words of the Bible (cf. Heb. 1:1–2; 1 Peter 1:16–21). The practice of cuddling up to God in all

manner of cozy ways that are not spelled out in Scripture (e.g., expecting God to speak to us directly by means of inner voices, impressions,
dreams, visions, checks, and prompting in one's spirit) can lead people
down dangerous paths. It's not that God is unable to do these things.
It's that He has told us to *seek* His will for our lives in the Bible.

2. Or, as I like to personalize it: loneliness is God's built-in alarm
system to let me know that it's time to draw nearer to Him.

3. The word used for "word" here is *rahma*, the spoken word—not
logos, the written word. The Spirit can most effectively use the Word
when it is on the tip of your tongue (because it is in your heart ready
to be used at a moment's notice).

Chapter Eight: There Goes My Security Thing

1. Even if those to whom you witness reject the gospel, your
witness can bring glory to God and you will be rewarded for faithfully
proclaiming the gospel.

2. Richard Baxter, *Baxter's Practical Work*, vol. 1, *The Christian Direc-
tory* (Ligonier, PA: Soli Deo Gloria Publications, 1996), 220 (updated
into modern English by the author).

Chapter Nine: Is Your Imagination Running Away with You?

1. Wayne Mack, *Homework Manual for Biblical Living*, vol. 1 (Phillipsburg, NJ: Presbyterian and Reformed, 1979), 176.

2. Such people never truly had saving faith. As John said of some of
his company, "They went out from us, but they were not of us; for if
they had been of us, they would have continued with us" (1 John 2:19).

3. D. Martyn Lloyd-Jones, *Spiritual Depression, Its Cause and Its Cure*
(Grand Rapids: Eerdmans, 1965), 86.

Chapter Eleven: What Good Comes to the Brokenhearted?

1. Jay E. Adams, *1 & 2 Corinthians*, Christian Counselor's Commentary
(Huntersville, NC: Timeless Texts, 1994), 129.

2. He overcame fear by loving his Lord and those for whom He had
died (cf. 1 John 4:8; 2 Tim. 2:9).

3. Adams, *1 & 2 Corinthians*, 130.

Chapter Thirteen: I Just Called to Say, "I *Don't* Love You!"

1. Lou Priolo, *The Heart of Anger* (Amityville, NY: Calvary Press, 1997). (This book addresses the problem of characterological anger in children. It has proved to be helpful for many adults as well.)

2. This is an introductory summary statement that identifies the result of the clamor before explaining its exact nature.

3. Note the public gathering of those whom Demetrius intended to infect with his bitterness.

Chapter Fifteen: Won't Be Cruel

1. The hurt can be real or imagined; it makes no difference. The result is the same. If you do not deal with it biblically, you will become bitter. If I hurt you as a result of my sin and you choose not to overlook it or cover it in love (Prov. 17:9; 1 Peter 4:8), you must follow Luke 17:3 and pursue me with the intent of granting me forgiveness, and I must repent. If you get your feelings hurt as a result of something I did that was not a sin, you must repent of your unbiblical thinking that caused you to be offended at something that was not a sin.

2. Lou Priolo, *The Complete Husband* (Amityville, NY: Calvary Press 1999), 104.

3. Proud people are especially prone to perceiving nonsinful pinpricks as though they were being stabbed through the heart.

4. Jay E. Adams, *From Forgiven to Forgiving* (Amityville, NJ: Calvary Press, 1994), 11–12.

5. *American Heritage Dictionary of the English Language*, 3rd ed. (New York: Houghton Mifflin, 1993).

6. If other individuals have a biblical need to know about the offense, you can lovingly urge the offender to confess to all necessary parties so that you will not be obligated to disclose anything to anyone.

Chapter Sixteen: Yesterday Wants More

1. Johannes P. Louw and Eugene A. Nida, *Greek-English Lexicon of the New Testament Based on Semantic Domains* (New York: United Bible Societies, 1988, 1989).

2. In a divorce, for example, removing certain things from the home cannot be done without punishing the children. The children

themselves may remind you of your ex, but you certainly cannot remove them from your life.

Chapter Seventeen: Will I Still Love You Tomorrow?

1. For an excellent treatment of this concept, see Jay E. Adams, *What to Do When You Worry All the Time* (Nutley, NJ: Presbyterian and Reformed, 1975).

2. For more examples of both false and despairing prophecies, see William Backus, *Telling the Truth to Troubled People* (Minneapolis: Bethany House), 129–31.

3. Johannes E. Louw and Eugene A. Nida, *Greek-English Lexicon of the New Testament Based on Semantic Domains* (New York: United Bible Societies), 1988, 1989).

Chapter Nineteen: I'm Nobody Till Somebody Loves Me

1. I am indebted to John Bettler and Jay Adams for the work they have done in unpacking the construct of self-image and repackaging it into biblical concepts.

2. For additional help in this area, obtain a copy of *What Exactly Is a Poor Self-Image,* available from Sound Word Associates, (219) 548-0933, http://www.soundword.com/index.html.

Chapter Twenty: Misheard It through the Grapevine?

1. A tiller is the mechanism (such as a steering wheel) that the ship's pilot uses to turn the rudder and steer the vessel.

2. Charles Spurgeon, *Metropolitan Tabernacle Pulpit*, vol. 11, sermon 647, preached on August 27, 1865.

Chapter Twenty-One: Won't Look Back

1. The things that Paul was "forgetting" were probably not his past sins, but rather those past "accomplishments" that he previously trusted would put him in good standing with God—"circumcised the eighth day, of the stock of Israel, of the tribe of Benjamin, a Hebrew of the Hebrews; concerning the law, a Pharisee; concerning zeal, persecuting the church; concerning the righteousness which is in the law, blameless" (Phil. 3:5–6).

2. The Bible speaks of a weak conscience (1 Cor. 8:7, 10, 12), a seared (or branded) conscience (1 Tim. 4:2), a defiled conscience (Titus 1:15), a conscience that is in need of cleansing from dead works (useless acts; Heb. 9:14), and an evil conscience (Heb. 10:22).

3. Lou Priolo, *The Heart of Anger* (Amityville, NY: Calvary Press, 1997), 179–80. For information on how to obtain a copy of this book, contact Calvary Press, Amityville, New York, 1-800-789-8175. For a thorough treatment of biblical forgiveness, see Jay E. Adams, *From Forgiven to Forgiving* (Amityville, NY: Calvary Press, 1994), also available through Calvary Press.

Chapter Twenty-Two: It's Your Party

1. It is possible that Job is not as envious as his words seem to indicate but is rather simply arguing the point to his three friends (who have wrongly concluded that he must have done something wrong; otherwise, the terrible things that had befallen him would not have happened) that God does sometimes allow the wicked to prosper and that they should therefore "lighten up" from their unrighteous judgments about his alleged sin.

Chapter Twenty-Three: Who Can You Turn To?

1. The Bible also lists a fair number of things that one may rightly love. The proper love of such eternal objects as God's Word (Ps. 119:140), wisdom (Prov. 29:3), biblical instruction (Prov. 12:1), and purity of heart (Prov. 22:11) are all elements of the greatest object of our love: God Himself!

2. There are occasions when I don't know what to say to some of my counselees because they are in so much distress. Without fail, when I turn to an appropriate passage of Scripture and read it to them, they receive a great measure of comfort. Never underestimate the tranquilizing power of God's Word!

3. Of course, there is a lot of weak and even heretical teaching out there. So if you have not yet learned to be discerning, you should ask those you know who are discerning for some recommendations.

Chapter Twenty-Four: Suspicious Mines

1. This particular Greek word for *jealous* is *zelos*.

2. By *attending sins* I mean particular sins that often join themselves to and lock arms with an initial sin, thus making it more difficult to remove from one's life.

Chapter Twenty-Five: Isn't That a Shame?

1. When these two fundamental sins join hands with the sin of worry, the results can be a paralyzing fear that can cause emotional depression—especially if it is allowed to so incapacitate the person that he or she stops fulfilling necessary responsibilities.

2. We must also guard against protecting our reputation inordinately lest it become an idolatrous desire that, like the love of money, will get us into all sorts of trouble.

3. These self-humbling phrases can be found in the following passages: 1 Kings 21:29; 2 Kings 22:19; 2 Chron. 7:14; 12:12; 33:12,19; 34:27; Ezra 8:21; Isa. 58:3; Matt. 23:12; Luke 14:11; 18:14; Phil. 2:8; James 4:10; 1 Peter 5:6.

4. An important principle in the Bible bears mentioning here. Either we humble ourselves voluntarily or God will humble us involuntarily. The choice is ours!

Chapter Twenty-Seven: Can't Smile Without Who?

1. Thomas Watson, *The Art of Divine Contentment* (Morgan, PA: Soli Deo Gloria Publications, 2001), 24–25.

Chapter Twenty-Eight: I Won't Last a Day Without Who?

1. Thomas Watson, *The Art of Divine Contentment* (Morgan, PA: Soli Deo Gloria Publications, 2001), 126–27.

Chapter Twenty-Nine: I Don't Need to Be in Love

1. Jeremiah Burroughs, *The Rare Jewel of Christian Contentment* (Edinburgh: Banner of Truth Trust, 1964), 35–36 (emphasis added).

2. I make a distinction between God's revealed will, which is found in Scripture, and His decreed will, which sometimes includes giving others the freedom to sin against Him. Christ's redemptive work on the cross, which God ordained in eternity past, involved certain individuals' committing murder. "Him, being delivered by the determined purpose and foreknowledge of God, you have taken by lawless hands, have crucified, and put to death" (Acts 2:23).

3. Paul, speaking as a prophet, is warning of the terrible persecution that Nero was about to inflict on Christians. At the time he was writing, the persecution was in its inception.

4. Burroughs, *Rare Jewel*, 226.

5. Ibid, 223–24.

Chapter Thirty: You Can't Hurry *Out of* Love

1. John E. MacArthur, *The MacArthur New Testament Commentary* (Chicago: Moody Press, 1983). See also Richard C. Trench, *Synonyms of the New Testament* (Grand Rapids: Eerdmans, 1983), 198.

Chapter Thirty-One: Someday Your Prince Will Come

1. If you are uncertain about what this means or about whether or not you are truly a Christian, if you've not yet done so, please take a moment to read Appendix C.

2. Even those Christians who are suffering with incurable or terminal illnesses have hope that someday God will let them out of the boxes of their fleshly tents (their physical bodies) and deliver them into the freedom (cf. Rom. 8:18–22) of their heavenly home ("a building from God, a house not made with hands, eternal in the heavens" [2 Cor. 5:1–4]).

3. Lou Priolo, *The Complete Husband* (Amityville, NY: Calvary Press, 1999), 233–35.

Appendix A: What Am I Doing the Rest of Your Life?

1. Pastoral counsel should *always* be sought whenever a believer finds himself facing the possibility of divorce.

2. This is not to imply that all divorced individuals would be wise to consider remarrying their ex. Indeed, in many cases it would be foolish or even sinful to do so. When a former spouse has truly repented, or when a divorce for unbiblical grounds has been obtained, reconciliation must be considered.

Appendix B: It's Not Too Late to Turn Back Now

1. See Proverbs 6:1–5 for general instructions about what to do when you make a foolish promise.

Appendix D: You Always Hurt the One You Don't Love

1. Some of the material in this appendix has been adapted and expanded from Wayne A. Mack, *A Homework Manual for Biblical Living*, vol. 2 (Phillipsburg, NJ: Presbyterian and Reformed, 1979), 35–38. Used by permission.

Appendix E: You Don't Have to *Say* "I Love You"

1. The list is sufficient but not exhaustive. There are other aspects of biblical love found elsewhere in the Bible that are not mentioned here (e.g., "there is no fear in love" [1 John 4:18]).

2. This phrase may also rightly be translated "love covers all things."

More relationship resources from
P&R PUBLISHING

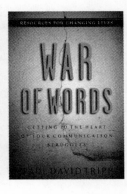

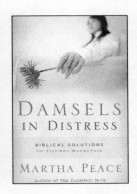

Full of Scripture, and challenging to the reader, *Pleasing People* takes aim at a problem common in all of us: the desire to be liked by others. But Priolo also wisely delineates when pleasing people is biblical.

"An extremely biblical and practical book to help the 'people pleaser.' Even if you think you do not have this weakness, you may be convicted that you do!"
—Martha Peace

Few of us really think about the power, the blessing, the gift, the effect, and the danger of our words. This book will make you think before you speak. Best of all, it will make you think of Him before you speak.

"You will be challenged, convicted, enlightened, and encouraged in this extremely important dimension of your relationship with God and with other people."
—Wayne A. Mack

Addresses ten issues that women face: the feminist influence, the role of women in the church, trials, gossip and slander, idolatrous emotional attachments, manipulation, hurt feelings, vanity, PMS, and legalism. The solutions are clear, God-honoring, and practical in their application.

"Clearly reveals God's principles for dealing with the common problems women face—first with others, then with themselves."
—Pat Ennis

More biblical guidance from
P&R PUBLISHING

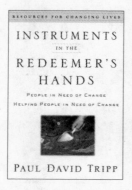

Following the example of Jesus, Tripp reveals how to get to know people at a deeper level and how to lovingly speak truth to them without breaking fellowship.

"Helps us help others (and ourselves) by giving grace-centered hope that we can indeed change, and by showing us the biblical way to make change happen."
—Skip Ryan

"Need people less. Love people more. That's the author's challenge. . . . He's talking about a tendency to hold other people in awe, to be controlled and mastered by them, to depend on them for what God alone can give."
—*Dallas Morning News*

"Ed Welch is a good physician of the soul. This book is enlightening, convicting, and encouraging. I highly recommend it."
—Jerry Bridges

Contentment is an essential Christian virtue, but it is one we often lack. William Barcley simplifies and restructures classic Puritan literature into accessible language to reveal the secret behind contentment.

"Planted in Philippians and watered with Puritan wisdom, this handbook on cultivating contentment unlocks one of the secrets of spiritual health and happiness. A rewarding study."
—J. I. Packer